# Joie Miami· Wh— — ıl
(

*Written by Nicole D. Peakler*
*Assisted by Nicole Levy*

## Table of Contents

"Sometimes the person you'd take a bullet for is the one aiming for you!"

To JoAnn Wainwright: After you hit rock bottom, there's nowhere else to go but up! Let's aim past the stars and head straight for the moon. Thank you for giving me this amazing opportunity to tell the life story of an incredible woman. I truthfully appreciate all of your motivation and encouragement.

To my Mother: Our lives have been like rollercoaster rides but sometimes less than thrilling. Regardless of the ups and downs, I love you Mom. Thank you for all you've done for me and my children.

To my children: You have always given me strength to continue on and believe in myself even when no one else does. You're the reason I do what I do. I would sacrifice everything just for you. I love you all!

Thanks to my Mother, JoAnn Wainwright and Gene Talarico for showing me love.

To my son, Gino and my daughter, Gabriella, I love you both so much.

Special thanks to my husband for sharing our crazy lives together.

My dear Uncle Tim, next to Gino, you have been the closest to a Father I have had. Thank you so much for loving me and my children.

To our angel, Samy, your encouragement to pursue this book and belief in it inspired me. Thank you.

I would love to send extra special thanks out to my daughter, Nicole Levy, and Nicole Peakler for taking on this project. You both have done such wonderful work and a terrific job.

To my son-in-law, you have always had my back and it truly means so much.

To my granddaughter, Gabriella and my grandson, Gino, you both are my heart and soul. You complete me. Thank you for being by my side.

To my lawyer, Andrew H. I have admired you and looked up to you for years.

To my family, friends and Lucy, I love you all so much.

To NYPD and NYFD: New York City is my home town. I thank you for your loyal support both during and after September 11th. God Bless you all!

Most of all, I would like to thank my special saints and God for pulling me through all of my demons.

## Introduction

When JoAnn Wainwright aka Joie Talarico called the Miami, Florida office of the Federal Bureau of Investigation in November 1989, she was a woman scorned and abandoned by the people she trusted most. Betrayal outweighed the code of loyalty. There was no longer honor among soldiers. She had been "fucked by the Mob without even a kiss!"

Having a home that was more like a battlefield due to her abusive father; Gene "Gino" Talarico appeared at a time in JoAnn's life when she needed it most. Like Prince Charming, he took her away from the destitution she knew and replaced it with tainted riches. It was her personal Cinderella story with a twist! Unfortunately, the happy ending she expected didn't come written like the fairy tale.

For fourteen years, JoAnn, known as Joie, had been the woman that stood strongly by the side of Gene Talarico, a Mafia soldier. She thrived off of a life style many would have quivered from. She was groomed to be an asset to Gene and his "employers" which turned out to be the South Florida Branch of the Chicago Mafia. For years she hosted gatherings, carried and laundered money, loaded planes to make drops, bought the apartments and cars for the "family" and kept their secrets. Her role in the Mafia grew to a liaison for Santo Trafficante. She saw heights many of the other Mob wives never knew.

The blood and sweat of loyalty, however, was washed away as Gene fell ill to cancer. Everything she worked so hard to build; the power, money and earthly possessions were stripped from her. She had been left out in the cold as a fallen and forgotten foot soldier and was made to survive on scraps. Joie had to count on the one thing the Mafia underestimated, her survival skills. With love now turned to hate, respect now turned to disdain and courage pumping in her veins, she returned the favor of spitting in the face of the Mob.

# Joie Miami

## Chapter One:  G'd Up

*My name is JoAnn Wainwright formerly Joie Talarico.  Though I have been known by many names, for fourteen years I was simply Joie, the woman of Gene Talarico (a Mafia soldier) and confidante of Hyman Larner, the head of the South Florida Branch of the Chicago Mob.*

*By the time I was strategically sitting in the hotel lobby as part of an undercover FBI investigation, Gene (the man I owed my life to) and Santo Trafficante (the man I respected most) were both dead and buried.  These two men, who I considered family more than my own blood, would be turning in their graves from my betrayal but I had been robbed of everything: my home, money and power.*

*Gene Talarico (the man I had lived with, protected and risked prison for) died of cancer, leaving me and my daughter Nikki, whom Gene raised as his own child without a cent.  Mafia code dictates whenever a soldier goes to prison or dies the family left behind is looked after for at least a year or two.  It was considered a severance pay package. I expected to receive this respect for all the shit I had done for them and all the secrets I had kept. Hell, I would have been happy with just five grand a month for six months! I had turned to all of Gene's associates for help and one by one they turned me down. One by one they left me and my child stranded in the cold. My reality was crystal clear. I had been fucked by the Mob without even a kiss! All the years of devotion and service had counted for nothing. With my refrigerator empty and rent three months overdue, I knew information would be my only currency. By the time I called the FBI building in downtown Miami in 1989, I had reached a level of desperation mixed with vengeance. There was no turning back but I didn't care. I was returning the Mafia's favor of slapping me in the face! I knew the risks I was taking. I knew the danger, but it was my only option for survival. I was abandoned by my own kind.*

I had barely stepped foot off the plane from Miami, Florida to Chicago, Illinois that mid-morning when two agents from the Federal Bureau of Investigation escorted me to a Lincoln Town Car. I was on my way to a hotel right outside of Chicago in Schaumburg and unaware of the whirlwind I was about to step in to. Awaiting my arrival, the FBI was busy setting up electronic recording and surveillance devices.

Entering the hotel room, I had a knot in the pit of my stomach. These were the men I worked so hard to evade and now I was working with them. Frank Morocco, head of the Chicago branch of the Federal Bureau of Investigation, and six other agents were inside the room and all eyes were on me. Morocco's stare was long and hard, one he'd probably perfected in a dungeon room for interrogations. It was as if he was trying to look right through to my soul. Greetings and salutations were sparse to none. These men were ready to get down to business. Something I was accustomed to and appreciated from working with the Mob.

Before the FBI started me on my assignment, they wanted to test just how legitimate I was in my level of information. Frank Morocco laid pictures on a table and asked me to identify the individuals in them. One photograph at a time, I confidently gave up names, ranks and the level of involvement each gangster pictured before me played with the Mafia. The "moment of truth" came when Morocco laid down two additional photos before me. One was of Salvadore Bastone. The other was of his brother Carmine. The two were a regular Cain and Abel act, always competing with each other for power. The brothers looked so similar in appearance. Often times when they were being investigated, agents had a hard time telling them apart. I picked up the first photo. Looking at it, I couldn't help but smile. "This one is Sal Bastone," I said. I had always been a little sweet on him. I thought of the many times we flirted together. Nothing ever came of it because he was married to a friend of mine. "This one is Carmine," I said with a bit of disgust. Sal may have been a cruel man but his brother was even more dangerous. I could see the faces of the agents as their excitement grew. "How are you so sure who's who?" said Morocco looking me plainly in the face. It was almost humorous to me to see how similar the FBI and the Mafia were when it came to suspicion. "Sal is better looking," I said. "She's definitely no flake!" blurted an agent.

Satisfied with my knowledge and responses, Morocco laid out the plan they had been so diligent in gearing up for. "Listen, we're trying to get Salvadore Bastone. We want you to call him and see if you can get him to meet up with you here. Do you think you can get him to come to you?" he said. "If I call him, he'll be here in five minutes," I said with a smirk. "What makes you say that?" Morocco said curiously. "Easy! My female charm and he trusts me," I said matter-of-factly.

Placing the hotel phone in front of me, Morocco gave me the "go-ahead". I felt hesitant at first but then I remembered how Sal was one of many associates of Gene's I begged and pleaded for help from. Not needing any assistance I knew what numbers to dial. Everything with the

Mafia is about following a chain-of-command. It didn't surprise me when I had to go through several people to finally speak with Sal directly. I told him I had won a lawsuit and came into a nice chunk of change. To peak his interest, I told him I was thinking of relocating to an expensive area of town off of Lakeshore Drive and was out there to check out real estate. I asked him if we could meet up for a drink and do a little catching up. The Mob is all about money and opportunity. His curiosity must have gotten the better of him. He agreed to meet at the hotel. I gave him the address and told him I looked forward to seeing him soon. After I hung up the phone, the room was in an uproar of celebration. "I don't believe it! We got him!"

I had seated myself by a window in the hotel lobby. I watched as the light from the sunset turned the horizon a vibrant orange color and seemed to paint the buildings in various shades of crimson red. The fall weather in Chicago was brisk with a touch of frost in the air at only 4 o'clock in the afternoon. Inside the lavish hotel lobby the climate was warm and much more inviting.

There was something almost harmonious about the lobby. From the cream-colored silk curtains that hung to the floor, the circular tables polished to a shine so deep I could see my reflection long enough to put on another coat of lipstick, to the Persian square carpet and the large ornate mirrors. The room had an air of elegance despite the discordant note of Feds all around me. Sitting on the other side of the criminal fence for once, I watched as they set the scene. Agents were everywhere. From the man reading the newspaper in the corner of the lobby, to the front desk clerks, even the doorman and bell hop were federal agents ready to pounce.

The Mafia was all about appearances and the FBI was fully aware. They spared no expense to make sure I looked the part. I have to admit one thing I have always enjoyed is being spoiled. I am after-all a woman. It had felt so familiar to sit in the lobby with an expensive pale blue silk blouse and charcoal gray Chanel suit that cost more than a full month's rent. Of course, let's not forget the accessories which my Mother always said brought out any outfit. I loved all of my new gifts from the G's right down to the Louis Vuitton purse with a hidden recorder inside.

I saw his face even before he entered the lobby doors. It was a face that was unforgettable. His image was one that had been permanently imprinted in my mind's eye from countless meetings, parties and dinners hosted by the Mafia. I had been around men like Sal Bastone for a good portion of my life. Men that were hungry for power. Men that didn't know the element of fear. Men that would gladly sell their souls to the Devil for a dollar! To me, there was nothing that could have been a bigger turn on.

Sal's face was dark and mysterious as the night but brutally sexy. With his sensuous full lips, thick wavy black hair, and almond-shaped brown eyes he had decadence in his appearance that could take a woman's breath away. My pulse raced from the sight of his presence partly from my overwhelming attraction but also because of what I was about to do to this man that I once befriended

.

Sal was supposedly out of commission and under house arrest for dealing cocaine out of a car dealership. That didn't stop him from going anywhere and doing anything he pleased. Being with the Mafia, I learned anyone can be bought even police and politicians at a fairly reasonable rate. Money had exchanged hands and Sal was as free as ever but he knew to watch hls back.

Seeing him walk through the lobby doors, I felt a tingling sensation go through my body. It was like being drunk or the feeling you would get being high for the first time. My heart began to beat a little harder. Outwardly, my smile didn't give a hint of the chaos I felt going on inside me.

Stage presence was about going into a trance and believing in the act, focusing on it, without the flicker of the eye. Something I had long since been groomed on. It was a part of my daily job description while working for Mob.

The grin on Sal's face from seeing me was wide and beautiful. I stood up to hug him. Sort of jokingly, he patted me down as if he was half feeling me up, half checking for a wire. I let out a small laugh. Though under the extreme circumstances, it still felt good to feel his firm arms wrapped around me. Nothing is more of a turn on for me then to feel the strength of a man. In my mind, I was thinking "This guy is so fucking hot! What the hell am I doing?!" I was fiercely attracted to him. Then I remembered how he had left me and my child destitute and to fend for ourselves, just like those other bastards I begged for help. All my financial troubles were about to be over. I was simply one click away. All I had to do now was turn on the device.

"Hey Joie. How's everything going?" he asked as we sat down. Facing him I could see there was still a touch of nervousness. No one else in the room would have been able to spot it but I knew he was wondering what the hell I was really doing in Chicago. "Things are going ok," I said as I unzipped my new purse and reached inside. I swiftly turned on the device,

17

pulled out a cigarette to cover my actions and said, "Mind if I smoke?" I lit it up and zipped up my purse so naturally that none would have been the wiser.

"So you wanted to see me?" he said. "Yeah Sal. I'm here for a few days on some personal business but I wanted to see you to get caught up," I replied. In a half hearted way, I actually was kind of happy to see him. After Gino died, I was cut off completely from everything and everyone I had known. It was nice to see a familiar face. "How are things out in Miami?" he asked casually. It was his attempt at making some friendly conversation. "They're starting to steam up. A lot of shit's going down. The feds have closed in on Noriega." He looked at me and said point blank, "If he ever talks, we're all fucked!" I knew he wasn't joking.

*Hyman Larner aka "The Old Man", boss of the South Florida Branch of the Chicago Mob in Miami, and Gene's former "employer", along with the rest of the Chicago crews were deeply involved with Colonel Manuel Noriega, the notorious drug running Panamanian dictator. Santo Trafficante, the man I was formerly a "liaison" to, ran Cuba before Castro. Santo was a very big opportunist and loved money. He had been careful with his* connections and was highly intelligent. For the right price, he had introduced Noriega to Hyman and the boys and left the business part to them. It was his way of keeping money flowing and his hands somewhat clean.

I fondly remember meeting Noriega and his family when they visited Miami. They made a stop at The Forge Restaurant on 41st Street in Miami Beach. The place had been a landmark in the city since the 1940s and had one hell of a steak! Whenever he came to town previously, he had always met with Larner. It was usually an extension of the business they were doing in Panama together from money fronted by the Mob. The working relationship stayed solid even after James Russell, a foot soldier for The Old Man, killed a Panamanian police office in a bar fight. Hyman paid big money to Panamanian officials to allow Russell to return to the United States. Russell was never allowed to step foot back in Panama again. When he returned to American soil, James Russell came to my home, handed me twenty thousand dollars and asked me to do him the favor of opening up a bank account under an assumed name so no one would know about it and he would have the money whenever he needed it.

I had learned James had a wife and several kids back in Panama. I asked Gene what was to become of the family and if they knew what James had done. "Who knows?" Gene said. "If they know what's good for

them they won't say anything or they'll end up the same way as the cop!" I
felt a chill go down the back of my neck. This was the heartless side of
Gene that I rarely got a glimpse of. But I knew if he had to, Gene would give
the order to kill Russell's wife and kids if they ever revealed what The Old
Man had done to get James out of Panama. After the night he showed up at
my home, I had never seen James Russell again. I tried several times to
contact him about the money but never got anywhere. I assumed he was
probably dead.

As a favor to The Old Man, Gene and I were asked to join them.
Colonel Manuel Noriega was a swarthy guy, with tough, pock-marked skin
and a strange aura around him. His wife was a refined looking Spanish
woman who was very attractive with her long flowing dark hair. She had
delicately balanced features and immaculate skin. All angles of her face
were measured out with the classic precision of a Swiss watch. She had the
look of true royalty. It was years later when I had learned that the elegant
looking woman had been arrested for stealing buttons off of Chanel suits!

That night out at dinner was the only time I had ever seen Gene
boisterous and showing off. Around a table in a simple restaurant, we all sat
like common everyday people eating, telling stories and sharing laughs like
old friends. They shared with us their plans to visit Disney World. Gene

*offered to drive them in his van with tinted windows. From that point onward, Gene had a connection to Noriega but he kept it very quiet. It was hush-hush even from me! Noriega came to my home about three or four times and I had barely even seen him.*

*From the conversations I was privy to and the little bit that my daughter Nikki picked up from the Spanish learned in school, I had known Noriega was involved with drug cartels based in Colombia. Panama was only the base of operations for bringing drugs into the United States. I learned more about these operations as my involvement with Santo began to grow and as Gene sent me out to do his dirty work.*

Sal and I gossiped for a little while about Noriega and The Old Man. I made sure that I sweet talked him just enough to establish the link between the Miami Mob boss and the Panamanian Colonel. I knew the FBI was listening so I started fishing around for anything else mob-related. "I wonder if Larner's going to leave from Panama now." I asked. "I don't know. I haven't spoken to the Old Man in years," Sal said and his body stiffened a bit.

To ensure they were getting the information they were paying me for, I dropped a few names like Joey DeVida and Vic Vita along with some of the other Miami and Chicago based lieutenants and foot soldiers. I knew Sal would take the bait and he did. The FBI now had their work cut out for them with the names and information Sal unknowingly provided. One thing I learned from being with Gene, Mob men loved to talk. Sal gossiped like an old woman about the Chicago crew. Who was going to prison, who was rising in the ranks, and Carmine, his "son of a bitch" brother as Sal liked to refer to him, was all among the topics of our conversation.

Carmine was always a touchy subject with Sal. I treaded lightly when it came to their relationship to be careful not to anger him. "That fuckin' brother of mine is back working for The Old Man," his body grew rigid again. "To think I helped that son of a bitch while he was in prison. Now he's fuckin' tryin' to take over my turf!" He slammed his fist on the table. Any other woman would have been startled, but I never budged. This was common from Sal when it came to talking about Carmine.

Sal opened up about Joey Ajuppo, aka Joey Doves, aka Joey O'Brien heading to prison for a long run. Sal busted his ass within his branch of the Mob and felt he was the next in line to be moved up and to take over Joey's spot. In his eyes, the power was his. Carmine had other ideas. Since Carmine had been released from prison for racketeering a while back without snitching on his crew, he felt he had made "bones" and had proven himself worthy of the position. He was willing to demonstrate his muscle to his own brother. To prove he was serious, Carmine convinced Joey DeVida, one of Sal's closest associates, to join his side. This made Sal furious and ready to strike back with revenge.

"I don't believe that Sal! After everything you and your wife did for him, for his family! How could he betray you like that?" I said with a hint of concern in my voice. "As far as I'm concerned, he's dead in my eyes. I have no brother!" Sal coldly said those words to me, and then smoothed his hands over his face as if to wipe away the disgust. "I know how you must be feeling right now to have family turn their backs on you," I said this to remind him of my betrayal from the Mob.

*Things weren't always so shrewd between the brothers. Back in the day, Sal and Carmine had been small time hoods together. They once busted into a card game in Chicago and held the players up. Little did they realize they were in the presence of real gangsters; some of the foot soldiers of the Chicago Mob, Hyman Larner and a few crooked cops had gotten together for a game of poker. Instead of killing them on the spot, The Old*

*Man was impressed with their enthusiasm. He turned to the brothers and*

*offered them jobs within his branch of the Mob. "There's a lot more money*

*to be made then what's in this room. Come work for me," he said and so*

*their establishment began. Larner wasn't disappointed in his new selection*

*of employees. The brothers were well connected in Chicago. It was through*

*those connections, The Old Man met several valuable acquaintances.*

Folding his hands in his lap, he looked me in the face as if to get

some sympathy. "Joie, I didn't even get the chance to go to Gene's funeral,"

he said. "Neither did I. Those bastards wouldn't allow it," I said with a touch

of sadness and a dash of disdain. Towards the end of Gene's life, as he had

grown more ill, his family and long lost son swooped in and took over

everything Gino and I worked hard to establish together. They were like a

plague of locusts devouring whatever they could.

Changing the subject, Sal complained that he was hot- meaning

the Gs were watching him because of his bust. None of his usual friends

would be around him. "Whatever happened to Sonny Pacini?" I asked.

Sonny had been Sal's runner. "He ain't with us no more, you know" He shot me a careful look. "What did you and the Old Man do, fire him?" "Like I said Joie, he ain't with us no more," Sal just stared hard at me. It was one of those looks that would cause goose bumps to go marching up your arms. In my mind, I said a little prayer for Sonny's obvious widow.

"What's happening with you now? House arrest I heard," we both laughed over it. "Yeah you know. Minor bump in the road," he said. "If I come out here you got any action for me?" I asked. Sal knew what I meant. Sal was very familiar in the things that I had done for Gene and Santo. He still dabbled in a few profitable illegal activities like running bingo and slot machines, laundering money, and doing some small time runs here and there. He told me his niece and nephew were already working for him and had it covered.

I noticed during our conversation Sal began leaning forward. He began to take long pauses before answering some of my questions as well. He put his hands on the table. I tried to over look the bizarre behavior to pump out some more information. Sal reached into his breast pocket and took out a cigarette. He looked me in the face and gave me an unnerving glance. Then without warning he snatched my Louis Vuitton purse, unzipped it and began rifling through it! "Hey Joie, let me borrow your lighter," he said. He kept his eyes on me. Slowly he took the lighter out of my purse, lit his cigarette, and placed the lighter back inside.

I froze in my seat. I could feel my stomach clenching itself in fear. My face felt flushed. He gave me a thin lipped smile as he placed my purse down. All I could do was sit there thinking I was about to die a painfully, humiliating death. I could feel the prickle of hairs standing straight on my neck. "Holy shit what have I done!" were the only words I could hear inside my mind. I gave him a searching look but his expression revealed nothing. If Sal felt the recording device, his poker face didn't show it and that frightened me more than if he would have just taken a gun out and pointed it at my face.

I desperately tried to pull myself together without giving away any secrets and keeping my composure. Though inwardly I was falling apart, on the outside I still appeared cool, calm and happy to be chatting with my longtime friend. "Listen, while I'm still in town why don't we go out for dinner?" I offered. Sal took a drag on his cigarette, crushed it out and plead business meetings all week. I knew that was his way of brushing me off.

He stood up to leave. I somehow managed to get to my feet and kissed him goodbye. "Glad I saw you Sal," I said. In a way, even through the fear and the diluted buzz of the Feds, I really was happy to have spent time with my friend. "I'm glad I saw you too, Joie," he said. He turned and started to walk towards the lobby doors. I stood there half watching and half waiting for him to turn around and shoot me execution style. He never did.

As he exited through the doors, I could feel myself exhale for the first time since he grabbed my purse. I could also feel my new gray charcoal suit was soaked with sweat all the way down my back and under my arms. I sat there in the lobby for a few minutes collecting both my thoughts and breath. I had kept company with some of the most dangerous and vicious criminals on this side of the Western Hemisphere, I had been in many life threatening situations, I had even risked going to prison, but this was by far my hardest mission yet. I had never been more scared as I was a few moments ago. To pull the wool over the eyes of someone I knew, who was my own kind and not once stumble and get caught was amazing. It took all the energy I had left to muster myself up and collect my thoughts. I knew I had to turn the evidence over to the Feds still. Just for a brief moment, I thought about walking out of the front lobby doors and down the street away from it all but I knew better. I knew if I had done that the Gs would have me hunted down in just a few minutes. They weren't about to let their newest informant slip through their fingers, especially after investing so much time and effort to collect the precious information I contained.

Coming off of the elevator, I could still feel my heart pounding a bit in my chest. I barely had the room key in the door when it swung wide open. Morocco was standing there waiting like a dog for its' treat. I handed him the Louis Vuitton and went for a glass of water. "Hey you did a great job! Superb! We're going to give you a little extra money for what you just pulled off Joie. We'll take good care of you and your kid," he said in a celebratory way. Taking a sip of the cool water all I could think about was how much I was glad it was over. I did exactly what I came to do for them. I felt out Sal. I provided the FBI with what they so desperately wanted- information. Now I was ready to get on with my life. Unfortunately, the FBI had other plans.

Joie Miami

## Chapter Two:  My First Family

Violence has never been a stranger to me.  Neither was making the best of a bad situation.  I guess that's why I was able to stay so strong in the lifestyle I was living.  By the time I met Gino Talarico in 1973, I was nineteen, a single mother and desperately trying to evade the wrath of my abusive alcoholic father *(if that's what you want to call him.)*

My sister Janice, the next to the youngest of four children in the household, was the first to "escape" as we liked to put it.  Our home was like a prison, we saw each other as captives being tortured by a sick fuck of a Warden.  At fifteen, Janice won a lawsuit from an accident and was given a large settlement.  She saw the money as a way of buying her own freedom.  Janice had a boyfriend who was Cuban and older then her.   He was head over heels for her and wanted nothing more than to marry her.  My sister may have been young but she was also very smart.  She knew our father loved two things in life, alcohol and money.  She struck a deal with the Devil himself.  After all, what was a few thousand dollars in exchange for freedom?  The last words I ever heard from my little sister was, "Just get out of the house!" We didn't see her again until later on in life when we were older and living lives much different from the ones we left behind.

I tried to escape once in a much different way from Janice. I was thirteen years old. It was New Year's Eve and the celebrating started early in my home in Detroit, Michigan. My mother and father had been drinking most of the day. I had made plans to go out with friends in the neighborhood to watch the fireworks go off. As I started towards the front door, my father came up behind me and grabbed my arm. "Where the hell do you think you're going?" he said. I could smell every drop of liquor on his breath. "Just going to watch some fireworks," I said. "You're not going anywhere! Sit your ass down!" and with force he threw me on the couch. I sat there for a moment collecting my wits and then slowly tried to inch easily off without him noticing. He went to go mix up another drink. I saw it as my big opportunity to make a break for it. Out of the corner of his eye he saw me. "Where the fuck are you going? Get the fuck back here bitch!" he yelled as I was running towards the door. Tears were welling up in my eyes. I knew once I was out of the house I had to come up with a plan to stay free.

My adrenaline kicked in and I ran as hard and as fast as I could through the snow to a friend's house a few streets over. It was freezing outside. I left the house so fast I didn't even grab a jacket. Gasping for air

30

and shivering, I banged at her front door. She and her mother opened it up and looked at me puzzled. "JoAnn! Are you ok?!" she said. I couldn't put the words together. My mind was swirling and my only thoughts were to be safe. They invited me to come inside. Shaking all over like I was coming down from a high, I sat on their couch. Her mother went to get me a glass of water. "Can I use your bathroom?" I said. "Sure, just take the stairs up and it's the first door to the right." They lived in a town house which was common in Detroit.

Inside that tiny room, my thoughts were all about what had just happened and what I knew I would have to face when I went back home. I couldn't help but burst out crying. My body was tired and my emotions were drained. I felt so numb and all I wanted was for it to end. This life wasn't worth living anymore. I couldn't take being my father's personal punching bag any longer. The bruises were becoming more impossible to cover up. I spotted a straight edge razor on the sink. It must have belonged to my friend's dad. I picked it up and looked closely at the sharp edge. It was so seductive to me. I barely felt the blade cutting in to my flesh. The blood felt warm dripping from my wrists on to the white tile of the bathroom floor. I felt the room start to spin and the weight of my body was too much for me to stand on my own. The room went dark and I fell to the floor.

Through the darkness, I could hear the sounds of beeping. The machine in the hospital room was keeping up with my heart beat. I heard muffled voices. Opening my eyes I saw my mother standing outside of the door way talking to a policeman. A nurse came in the room. While changing my bandages she said, "You know you gave us a good scare!" I just looked at her. I didn't know her name and never really cared to find out. I was more disappointed that I was still alive. In my mind, death was the only real peace I could have.

The nurse left the room and informed my mother and the officer that I was awake. With a face more pale than mine and mascara streamed down the sides, my mom sat beside my bed. She threw herself on top of me and was sobbing. "Why? Why would you do this to yourself? Why would you do this to me?" she said through the tears. I wanted to tell her it was because she was too scared to protect her children. I wanted to say it was because of the bastard of a man that was my so-called father. I wanted to say because it was better than living another second in that torture chamber of a home. All I could do was lie there silent.

A few days later I was released from the hospital with the stitches and bandages still on my wrists. My mother escorted me back to the house where my siblings were awaiting my arrival. As we entered the front door, I spotted my father sitting in his usual chair with a beer in his hand. He took long slow sips and kept his eyes on me but never once said a word.

My apparent suicide attempt didn't change much in the house. For about a week, things seemed quiet and settled down. People looking in from the outside would have never been able to tell the type of drama that would soon unfold. My mother did what she could to keep a close watch on me and my siblings. She didn't want another incident to occur. I felt sorry for her. She was married to a man that was cruel and treated her and her children like we didn't have the right to live like human beings. Honestly though, how sorry can you really feel for someone who refused to leave her abuser? You know the saying, *"You can only keep animals caged and backed up in a corner for so long before they attack!"* I guess my father had to learn it the hard way.

In 1967, my father rented a fully furnished home which was actually nicer than where we previously lived in Detroit. It was his way of offering us a fresh start. How can something be fresh when it still stinks like shit? Only a few months went by before he was back to drinking heavily and his demon side resurfaced. My mother noticed he began to take off for days at time never letting anyone know his whereabouts. The landlord came by once, he informed my mother that the rent has not been paid for over two months. We were behind in rent over five hundred dollars. Back in the sixties that was a lot of money. She was completely in shock. We had just gotten settled in to our new home with such high hopes and once again reality was smacking us in our faces. The landlord gave us an additional three weeks as a courtesy. After he left, my mom was on the phone trying to contact everyone she could to see if anyone had known where my father was. She even contacted as many family members as she could to see if anyone could help us come up with the money that was owed. The most she was able to get together was fifty dollars. She was devastated and couldn't stop the tears from flowing. "Why did he move us here? We were fine in New York. I could have gotten Welfare there. I knew people to find work. I could have helped our family to be provided for. He moves us here and takes off. We have to fend for ourselves. This is not the life we were supposed to have!" I had never seen her so grief stricken. She had cried tears before but there was something different in her eyes this time. Something was building up.

A few nights later my father came home. He had gone out with some of the men he had met from his new job to a bar that was only four blocks from our home. It was late but I could hear his and another man's voice outside the front door while he stumbled for keys. *I had the habit of staying up as late as I could to keep watch over the others while they slept. It was a small gesture of love but to them it meant a lot.* Since he couldn't find his keys, he started banging on the front door. He seemed to get enraged because we weren't moving fast enough to open it. My parents' room was downstairs. I could hear my mother going to the door. She could barely turn the lock when he busted through. I rushed from my bedroom to the top of the stairs to see what was going on.

"Stupid motherfucker!" he shouted. "What's wrong with you?!" my mother screamed. His companion wasn't too far behind in the door way. My father smacked her in the face and she fell back. "Shut up bitch! You're a useless piece of shit!" he said as he stumbled around drunk. His insults were just getting started. "You're old and washed up! I need some new blood! Where are those daughters of yours!?" he said. My mother was on the couch stunned from how hard he hit her. His friend was leaning up against the door frame. My father started towards the stairs. I saw his rabid face and scrambled towards the bedroom door. I banged on the walls and doors as hard as I could to wake the others from the impending doom that was about to unleash.

My mother got up from the couch and went racing towards the stairs. "You sick Mother Fucker! Get away from them!" she screamed. "Stay away from my babies!" She grabbed his legs and started reaching for the back of his pants to pull him down the steps. He started kicking at her, striking her in the face again but this time with his foot. His kick must have hit the switch to my mother's rage. The animal was about to strike back!

"No! No! You bastard!" she started hitting him again. She was punching him in the back of his head. He turned around and they fell down the stairs on top of each other. That's when she spotted me. "JoAnn, get me a knife!" "For what?!" I was startled. She had never told me to do something like that before. "Just do it!" she said. He got on top of her and began punching her. I ran down the stairs as fast as I could past my father. His friend was on-looking in a daze. I grabbed the butcher knife from the kitchen drawer. As they rolled around on the floor somehow my mother managed to get on top. "Give me the knife!" she bellowed. I ran over and thrust it into her hands. In one swift motion, she stabbed him in his bicep! She pulled it out and stabbed him again and again. He was squealing like a pig! "You sonuvabitch! I'm going to kill you!"

His friend's eyes went wide from what he was witnessing. He fell backwards through the front door and took off running down the front stairs and up the street. He was screaming for help. Everyone from the neighborhood could hear his cries. I looked out the front door and saw the lights going on in each neighbors home one by one.

"I don't want no man in my house! I hate you! You bastard, I want you dead!" She was still holding the knife. She stuck it in him one final time. My brother and sisters were at the top of the stairs watching in fright as she jabbed the knife in his wrist. I was at the foot of the stairs. My mother got off of him and revealed the knife buried deep in his flesh. Blood was pooling on the floor. He was screaming in pain. With his other hand, he pulled the knife from his wrist and dropped it to the floor. He held his hand close to his body trying to get the blood to stop. He was shown no mercy.

I heard the familiar sound of sirens coming up the street and could see the flashing lights. The red and blue colors brightly lit up my doorway. I looked at my mother who was crying her eyes out on the floor. I looked at this beast that was a man. I heard the footsteps vastly approaching. I knew my mother was in enough pain and suffering all she could stand. I knew if they arrested her we would probably never see her again. I didn't want my siblings left with that vile beast of a man. In an instant, I picked up the knife. I already had blood splatters on my night gown from being in close range when my mother stabbed him. All the officers saw was my mother crying, my father bleeding uncontrollably on the floor against the wall and me standing there in front of them with the knife. They asked me what happened. I told them it was me. I told them I snapped and couldn't take the abuse anymore. I told them how he smacked my mother and kicked her in the face while she was trying to protect us. They called for an ambulance to come to the scene. Everything went silent in my hearing after that. I could see what was going on around me. I could feel the handcuffs being placed on my wrists and being led to the police car. I could even see my mother's face as she mouthed the words, "She didn't do it!" I just couldn't hear anything. It was all happening in slow motion. When the door to the car slammed shut it was like the world sped up again. I could hear the sounds of the radio and the officers calling in my arrest.

Word of what happened spread quickly throughout the neighborhood. Without warning, our landlord and some people he hired were soon grabbing our personal belongings and placing them out on the street like it was trash. He made the decision to evict us. Neighbors began to come outside and watch. Hearing the cries from my little sister and seeing my mother's distraught face, a woman by the name of Karen McCaskel came forward. She was new to the neighborhood and wanted to help. She was an angel in that moment and offered my family shelter until my mom could get us back on our feet.

Without my father around, my mother became productive. She eventually was able to get help from Welfare and found us a townhouse apartment in downtown Detroit near Jefferson Avenue. Soon I was released back in to her custody and our lives seemed so peaceful. Our apartment was small but I loved how my Mom had made it seem cozy for our little family. It was in that quaint home that our family experienced happiness for a brief time. All good things come to an end though. My father found out where we were living and showed up one night at our back door. Tears in his eyes he pleaded his case to our mother. He professed his guilt and how sorry he was but even crocodiles can shed tears. She took him back against our objections. Soon the games he played and the abuse was back in full swing.

Throughout my childhood, I was never convinced Joseph Spondike was my biological father. How *could* he have been when he treated me this way? How could any of us have been his real children with the abuse that we suffered by this demented man? I had never heard of any father hitting their child so hard they went through a second story window like he did to me! Father was a title of respect and it was something he didn't deserve. People say his ways were passed on by his mother. She was even more sadistic and cruel. From time to time when we visited her, she displayed just how heartless she could be. The abuse we experienced from her made our home lives look like a walk through Disneyland. My only thought was both of them should be put down like rabid dogs. I prayed daily for them to meet their "Day of Reckoning" but it was just not yet in the cards.

When I was twelve years old, my suspicions of not being a part of the sick gene pool my so-called father and grandmother were from became facts. I found out Joseph Spondike was my mother's second marriage. In fact, my mom Genevive Wanda Spondike was formerly Mrs. Paul Gallo, of the infamous New York Mafia. I had overheard from one of my grandmother's conversations that I was the byproduct of my mother's failed marriage. I never understood all of the whispers and stares when I was younger until I met Paul Gallo. I could have been his twin. It was during that meeting that I worked up the courage to ask him, "Are you my father?" Holding my face to look up at him, he smiled and said "I *could* be your father." There was so much I wanted to ask; so much I wanted to say, so many emotions running high. Before I could speak another word, he and my mother parted ways and I never saw him again. I still have the question of, "If I was his child then why leave me in the hands of a twisted bastard to torture me?" I felt the men of my life completely let me down. They displayed to me that women were not valued or appreciated. We were merely possessions and toys that could be played with; abused, destroyed and tossed away. That was a hard lesson to learn at an early age. At the same time, it placed a hunger inside of me that was for vengeance. In my mind, I was simply storing data to remember later so I could show the son-of-a-bitches who the "Top Dog" was going to really be!

My sister's words always rang loudly in my memory. She was right. I needed to get the fuck out of that house. It wasn't so much for my safety now, but for my child's well being. Nikki, my unexpected little angel, was my life. While I was working at a nursing home as an assistant, I had gotten pregnant. I knew I wanted my child from the moment I found out she was growing inside of me. Nikki was every drop of love I could ever feel in one tiny bundle of joy. I would have done anything to take her away from that wretched house. Hell, I didn't give a shit if I had to be a hooker; it still would have been better than to live there. If that would have been the only way out, then it was the route I was willing to travel. Besides, there wouldn't have been any abuse to my body that I had not already been through. In the end, I took a minimum wage job as a waitress at a diner after my father moved our family to Hollywood, Florida in 1973. That's when Gene walked in and my new life started.

Joie Miami

## Chapter Three: Being Made

Most women have the vision of Prince Charming arriving on a white horse; mine arrived in a black Cadillac. Gazing out of one of the front windows to the diner, I spotted a man, fifty-something years old and sexy as all hell stepping out of a brand new car. Two other men were with him but couldn't hold a match to his presence. His hair was dark with a distinguished touch of silver. He had a rugged face with olive skin, a Roman style nose and dark bedroom eyes. He was wearing thick gold chains around his neck with the matching rings and bracelet, a double-knit shirt with perfectly matching slacks, spotless Bally shoes and the confidence of someone half his age to tie it all together. He was smooth like butter and I was already melting.

"What are you over here staring at girl?" said Dee Dee. She was a waitress at the restaurant as well. Early on we hit it off and became somewhat close. Dee Dee had moxie like me, along with gorgeous natural red hair and a body that should have been on a pin-up poster somewhere for men to gawk. She reminded me of a young Lucille Ball sometimes with the way she wore her hair up. She looked out the window and spotted the car and the men. "Oh, I see what we're lookin' at!" she said in a sing-song type of way. "Damn girl, you sure know how to pick 'em don't you!" "What do you mean?" I asked kind of puzzled. "They're what you call Grade A hoods! They're the real thing Joie. *Very well connected.* Al Capone's boys! Get it?!" she said letting out a giggle. "They're from the Mafia?" "You got it Joie. That's Gene "Gino" Talarico and his boys and they eat here. Amazing isn't it? All that money and power and you come to a nickel and dime restaurant for lunch!" Her words were more intriguing to me then a warning. They came inside and sat at a booth. From close range you could feel the aura of power oozing from them. It was like a magnet drawing me close.

Dee Dee made her way over to their table and was handing them menus and taking drink orders. I noticed she gave me a quick look with a smile. She shook her head to something Gino said and walked away from the table. Bouncing her way over to me, "two coffees and a Coke," she said. "What?" "Their drink order. Two coffees and Coke. They must have spotted you lookin' at them through the window. They asked for you to be their waitress. So strap on your big girl boots babe and get to it!" I loved her energy and playful nature. She definitely made it a fun place to work. She went ahead and fixed the coffees. I poured the Coke. "Ok girl, let me look at you." She did a once over and said, "Beautiful. Now knock 'em dead!" She laughed and handed me the tray with a pat on my ass.

Heading over to the table, I felt a hot flush run through my body but played it off with a smile. "Here's your drinks fellas. Who has the Coke?" I asked. "That would be me Doll," said Gino in a tough Chicago style accent. "The name is Joie, handsome," I said as I placed the drinks on the table. "I'm Gene but my friends all call me Gino, since we're exchanging names now," he said with a flirtatious grin. His attitude was a mixture of cockiness and confidence. "So what'll it be for you Gino?" "I'll take a grilled cheese baby. I mean, Joie." It was cute how he was playful. The others gave me their orders and I turned to walk away. I could feel his eyes checking me out and gave him something to watch as I swished my hips from left to right. I never felt I was very pretty but I knew I had a hot body and wasn't afraid to use the gifts God gave me.

Returning to the table to serve Gene and his friends their lunch orders, I noticed that one of the guys had a lump under the front of his jacket. I looked a little closer as I placed his order down and realized it was the shape of a gun. Instead of feeling scared, I wondered what it felt like to hold something so powerful. Gene noticed my glance and to play it off he said, "How old are you Joie?" "I'm old enough," I replied in a none-of-your business attitude. "Yeah, I have a son 'round about that age." He grinned at me again. He had a gorgeous smile that seemed to make me forget my surroundings. "Is there anything else I can get you guys?" "No Doll. We're good," said Gene and he looked at me waiting for a response. I just winked then walked away.

Dee Dee was standing behind the counter and saw everything. She gave me a look that said *"Way to go girl!"* all over it. Approaching the counter, she said quietly to me "he's been watching you since you walked away from the table." Mission accomplished. Gene and his boys finished their food, got up from the table and started towards the door. I noticed Gino stopped Dee Dee and they exchanged words. She was smiling and I felt jealousy growing inside of me. I began to think I overplayed my position. She strutted over to me with a big grin. "What are you so happy about?" I said holding in every drop of jealousy I could. "Oh, I don't know. Maybe because he asked me what kind of things you like so he can impress you with his big Mafioso style," she said and laughed. "Girl, you should have seen your face. You would have thought you were ready to kick my ass!" "Well I kinda was," I replied and chuckled with her a bit. "You definitely caught his attention Joie," she said and I knew she was right.

Shortly after Gene and his boys left, the door to the restaurant opened up. In walked a man about 80 years old and wearing a Fedora style hat and matching blazer. His shoes were shined so brightly the lights of the restaurant were reflecting off of them. He sat down at the counter. Dee Dee went over to serve him. I took a little break back by the window to think a bit about Gene. I had a man I was already seeing for a few months but it wasn't too serious and he definitely was nothing like Gene. Dee Dee came over to the window. "Geez! What is it with you?" "What do you mean?" I asked. "All the big wigs want a piece of you." My face turned red. "You're not saying that guy over there asked about me are you?" "He asked me who the blonde was. I told him your name was Joie." I felt a bit embarrassed that someone of his age group had an eye on me. "He said he wanted to take you out," said Dee Dee with a grin. "Oh my God! What did you say?!" "I said you would love to but you were into women. Problem solved!" she busted out laughing. I never expected a response like that and couldn't contain my laughter. Dee Dee told me his name was Tony Gobel. He was very well respected and known in the neighborhood. He was also old enough to be my grandfather. I was always sweet to him every time he came back in but I guess what Dee Dee had said to him about me left him a little standoffish. I didn't mind. It was one less thing to worry about.

Being a single Mom was never easy but it was a choice I made. I met my daughter's father while working as a CNA at a nursing home. I had big dreams of becoming a full fledged nurse. My dreams were short lived though. I didn't have the financial backing to finish my education and I got pregnant with Nikki at an early age. Even though some nights I would be up late taking care of her exhausted beyond belief, I loved every minute of it. She was the only person in my life that I felt pure love from. After a long night with my little girl, I woke up the next day 30 minutes late with the alarm clock buzzing by my head. I jumped out of bed and scrambled to put my uniform on and fix my hair. Nikki was in her crib passed out and I was grateful for such a small miracle. Rushing down the stairs passed my mother; I gave her a kiss and headed for the door.

When I got to work Dee Dee was serving a table with her hair in its usual style. She really was a knock out. "Where have you been?" she said as she walked passed me to put the order in. "I'm sorry. I was up late with my kid and overslept." "It's cool. I was just hoping that if you didn't show maybe I could take all the gifts home with me." "Gifts?" "Yeah! A couple of Gino's boys came by here and dropped some presents off for you. Of course if you don't want them, I would be more than happy to take them off your hands," Dee Dee said in a playful tone. "Are you serious?!" I said excitedly. "Take a look. They're under the counter." I was in such shock. I wasn't used to having someone randomly buy me things. To my amazement, there was a bottle of perfume, Chanel Number 5, and carton of cigarettes. I couldn't help myself. I opened the top of the perfume bottle, took a sniff of the wonderful fragrance and dabbed a little behind my ears and on my wrists. It made me feel so beautiful and like a woman.

A few days later, while taking an order at a table of some obnoxious assholes that came in more to observe the women rather than to eat, I happened to look up and seen through the window a brand new Oldsmobile in front of the restaurant. It was top of the line and chocolate brown with tinted windows. My curiosity got the better of me so I watched until the doors opened up. Out stepped Gino looking just as sexy as the first time we met. He headed towards the front door to come inside. I acted as if I hadn't seen him and went behind the counter to place the order for my table. As I turned around, he took a seat at the counter. "So what's a guy gotta do to get a cup of Joe around here?" he said jokingly. I couldn't contain my smile from growing across my lips. "Cream and sugar with that?" I asked. "You got it doll. Excuse me, I mean Joie" he said while giving me a little wink. I loved how he flirted with me. I placed the coffee in front of him with a saucer of creamers and sugar. "Here you go love," I said and turned to get the food from my order.

Taking the tray over to the table I knew he was watching so I made sure to give it my best strut. I could feel his eyes all over my backside. "Here's your food fellas. Would you be needing anything else?" I said as I placed the food down on the table for them. "Yeah babe!" one said and smacked my ass "How's about your phone number?!" he said and was laughing. I stayed as calm as I could but the anger was welling in the pit of my stomach. Before I could say anything, Gino was standing behind me. "Excuse me fellas," he said and their eyes all locked on him. Gino was well known and the fact that he was standing in front of their table must have taken them by surprise. Their eyes grew wide and for the first time since they walked through the door they were silent. "Yes sir" said one of them with a look on his face like he was about to either throw up or shit himself. "She's a good woman. She works hard for her money. She's respectful and doesn't deserve a few meatheads like you to come in here and act like dogs fighting over a bone. Now, I know you have mothers and they wouldn't be too pleased to see you in here being rude. So, I suggest you apologize to this lovely woman on your own free will before I make you apologize by mine," he said it so straight-to-the-point that they came up quick with the apologies. "One more thing fellas, be sure to leave her a good tip," he nodded his head at them as if to make sure they understood what he was saying and went back to the counter. The dumbfounded looks on their faces was more than enough of a tip for me. They sat quietly eating their food. From such a small interaction I could feel his power and it was enough to have my hormones in overdrive.

I went over to where Gino was sitting sipping his coffee. I looked at him and all I could think about was how much I wanted him but I knew he was about respect so I kept it to myself. "You get the gifts I sent?" he asked as if nothing just happened. "Yeah I got them. Thank you. The perfume smells so beautiful. You really didn't have to buy them for me though." I really was appreciative but no one had ever bought me anything so expensive before. I didn't know how to truly accept the gifts. "Why not? You're a nice woman. You deserve nice things," he flashed a grin at me that made my toes curl from excitement. I loved how he saw me as a woman, not a girl. "So how's your night going?" he asked and turned a little bit to look back at the guys at the table. They were shoveling the food in their mouths and never once looked up. "It's going ok. Thank you for saying something to them by the way," I said. "It's nothing," he shrugged it off.

Gino was taking a sip of his coffee when I spotted a diamond ring on his finger. "You married?" I asked inquisitively nodding my head towards his hand. "No it's just a ring. I like it, so I wear it." I learned that Gino always had a very matter-of-fact personality once we got to know each other better. "So when are you gonna ask me out?" I blurted out. It took all he had to not spit the coffee from his mouth while holding back his laughter. "Ask you out? I'm an old man! What do you want with me?" he seemed so surprised. I could see him slightly blushing from my words. "What does any woman want with a man?" I replied. I knew a man like Gino would be good for me. He was rugged with a touch of class. He was like a gentle beast with me. "You're serious huh?" I could tell I captured his interest. "Yeah why not? I'll take you out. Write down your address and I'll pick you up on Friday at eight o'clock." "But I got a shift Friday and it's my birthday." "Don't worry, it'll be covered." He said things in such a manner that I truly believed if he wanted the world to stop spinning all he had to do was say it. Suddenly, I realized I didn't really know this man so a little anxiety hit. "Would you mind if my friend Dee Dee came with us? You know, for a little moral support." "You mean for protection." He winked at me. "Yeah sure Joie, bring her along. Just make sure you're both ready and looking beautiful as usual," he said graciously. "I gotta get going. See

52

you Friday." His suave personality truly demonstrated he was someone that never missed a beat. He turned and looked at the table of morons from earlier. They scrambled around at the table, threw some cash down and hurried out the door. He waited until they were gone. "Ok doll, take care." He tipped his hat at me and left out of the door behind them. I watched out of the window as he got into his car and pulled off. Walking over to clear the table, I noticed the guys left enough to cover the bill and an extra fifty dollars. I couldn't help but laugh.

That night I eagerly went home and couldn't wait to tell my mother about Gino and our upcoming date. It was nice to open up and talk about guys with her for a change. Gino wasn't just any guy though and I knew it. Having her there for guidance was the first time I truly felt the "Mother, Daughter" bond between us. "What am I gonna wear, Ma?" I moaned as I rambled through my closet. "I gotta have something elegant. This guy is not some street punk. I wanna look extra beautiful." "Don't worry JoAnn, we'll get something together," she said reassuringly. "I got a little extra cash your father doesn't know about. We'll go and get you something nice." She looked at me in a way that made me feel loved. It's the look a mother gives when she realizes her little girl is all grown up.

We got in the family car and went to a nearby small strip of stores. Rack after rack of pants, shirts, dresses we searched. I felt excitement grow like a high school girl getting ready for prom. "JoAnn, this is the one!" she said as if she found a prize. It was a little black dress with lace around the middle. It was basic but very classy looking. The price tag said $12.99, which meant it was in our budget. She told me to try it on. While I was in the dressing room putting it on, she handed me a pair of heels and necklace to tie it all together. "Let me get a look!" she said anxiously. I stepped out of the dressing room. "Oh JoAnn, you're gorgeous," she said with a little bit of tears working up in her eyes. Anyone in the store could see she was a proud mom. I looked in the mirror at myself. My mother came up behind me and played with my hair. "Maybe if we put it up in French roll or a bun?" "Yeah Ma, I would like that," I said smiling. We paid for the items and went home giddy.

The night of the date, my mother was helping me to get ready when the door bell rang. She was putting the finishing touches on my hair when we heard the bell again. "I'll get it," she said "You just stay focused on getting ready." She went downstairs. I was dabbing a little bit of the Chanel Number 5 Gino had given me on the sides of my neck when I heard my mother excitedly shout "Oh my God!" I went rushing to the top of the stairs.

Looking down, I saw a delivery boy with two dozen long stemmed pink roses standing in the door way. "JoAnn! They're for you!" I went racing down the stairs. I never received flowers from a man before. My mother and I were both stunned. She took the flowers in to the kitchen to get a vase and told me to finish getting ready. By now there was a fever pitched of anticipation and enthusiasm for the date. I couldn't wait to see what else he had in store.

After putting the finishing touches on my outfit and hair, I came back down to find my father slumped on the couch drunk with the television going. The flowers Gino had sent were arranged in a beautiful crystal vase in the center of the living room. They put a smile on my face. I was keeping a close eye on the window for his car. Soon I saw approaching head lights and the familiar Oldsmobile, knowing I didn't want him to step foot in to the house and have my father leave an unforgettable impression, I stepped outside of the front door before he made it up my stairs. I acted surprised to see him because I didn't want him assuming I was desperate.

"Hey! How are you? Did you find the place ok?" I asked. "Wow Joie! Look at you. You're breathtaking," he said and gave me a good once over. My mother came out of the house behind me holding Nikki fresh from a bath and smelling baby sweet. "And who is this gorgeous woman?" he asked. My mother blushed. With her cheeks flushed, she couldn't hold back her girlish smile. "I'm JoAnn's mom," she said. "Pleased to meet you." "The pleasure is all mine," said Gino and he took my mother's hand in his and gave her a little bow. It was cute to see him interact with her that way. With everything my father put her through on a daily basis; it made me smile to see her get treated like a woman. His eyes soon went to Nikki. She was wearing a buttercup yellow pajama. Her brown, wavy hair was still wet from her bath and slicked back. Her big Betty Boop eyes were staring right at Gino. He was so enchanted with her. He reached out and shook her tiny hand formally. "Hello gorgeous!" he said softly to her. Nikki giggled and buried her face into my mother's shoulder. He was charmed right down to his socks with her. I couldn't believe it. Here was this well known and feared man standing on my front steps cooing at my little girl. Gino gallantly won my mother's heart that night. "Well ladies," he said to my mom and Nikki "we must be off but I wish you both a wonderful night." I gave Nikki and my mother both a kiss and we were on our way to Dee Dee's place.

Sitting nervously next Gino, I wondered where we were heading. I started envisioning all these lavish places. We picked up Dee Dee and were off again. "So Gino, where exactly are we going?" I asked because the curiosity was getting the better of me. "Yeah. Where are we going? You know curiosity can kill a cat!" Dee Dee said from the backseat. "Good thing you're not cats," said Gino with his usual grin. There really was something about his smile that just caught my eye. "It's a surprise! Don't women like surprises?" he said jokingly. "Of course we do. We also like diamonds too!" teased Dee Dee and she gave me a wink.

It didn't take too long to get to our destination. We pulled up in front a small Italian restaurant called *Capra's*. It was a little "mom and pop" place off of Biscayne Boulevard in Miami. I was a little disappointed from the look of it at first until we stepped out of the car. The valet opened the door and suddenly I felt like I was on the red carpet of a Hollywood event. People in the neighborhood, the valet staff and even waiters were coming outside just to greet Gino. They made it feel like he was the celebrity of the night and Dee Dee and I were his escorts. Everyone came to shake his hand and greet him. "Hey Gino! How you doing? Look at you and these beautiful women!" Dee Dee and I couldn't wipe the smiles off of our faces. "Dee Dee have you ever seen anything like this before?" I asked. "Just go with it Joie," she said full of excitement.

We finally made our way inside the restaurant. The place wasn't fancy. It had round tables covered with plain white table cloths. Red velvet curtains with gold tassels surrounded the windows. Oil paintings of various places in Italy were scattered among most of the walls. To the naked eye,

57

this was just a little "hole in the wall" but what gave it away were the black and white autographed photos behind the counter where the cash register was located. Pictures of Anthony Quinn, George Raft, Joe DiMaggio, Marlon Brando, and Frank Sinatra were just the tips of the iceberg. All I kept thinking was "Holy Shit!" as my eyes went from frame to frame.

Before we could take our seats, the owner Vincent came out to greet us. "Gino! So nice to see you! And look at this, you brought me some lovely ladies," he took our hands and kissed them. I could feel my face flush from embarrassment. I was never used to such attention. He led us to a table by a window. I looked around and saw musicians strolling from table to table. "Please have a seat. I'm gonna have the best on the menu sent to your table. What would you like to drink?" he asked. Gino and Dee Dee both ordered wine. I was still under age so I asked for a Coke. After taking our drink orders he was off to the kitchen and was speaking in Italian to those along the way. I tried my hardest to get comfortable but people kept coming to say hello to Gino, who was dispensing "tips" as he called them. Soon our table was filled with salad, bread, wine, pasta and seafood. I didn't know if we were expected to eat it all or if there were people joining us. Dee Dee was having a ball. Gino was not a shy eater at all. I was so nervous I couldn't even taste anything.

As we were finishing our meal, Gino finally cleared his throat and looked at me. "So Joie, didn't you say it was your birthday?" He was looking at me in such a concentrated way. I felt butterflies in my stomach. Of course, it could have also been all the pasta making its way to its' final destination. "Yeah," I replied and noticed Dee Dee letting out a tiny giggle behind her wine glass. "What's going on?" I asked puzzled. Then I spotted out of the corner of my eye a huge white cake frosted with pink and yellow roses and bordered by green leaves being wheeled in. The cake read, "Happy 20th Birthday Joie!" Suddenly the musicians, waiters, owner and other patrons of the restaurant were singing "Happy Birthday!" and it was all for me. All I could get out was "Oh my God! No one's ever done this for me!" Gino put his arm around my waist and pulled me close and said, "Well, I'm doing this for you. Happy Birthday, babe!" he said and then kissed my cheek. "Now blow out the candles" shouted Dee Dee "and don't forget your wish!" Blowing out the candles all I could think about was how much I didn't want this night to end but I knew reality would set in. In the meantime, I enjoyed my cake.

As we were preparing to leave the restaurant everyone gathered together for their goodbyes. The night felt like it was right out of a movie. Nothing could have made things more special. "Did you have a good time?"

Gino asked after we settled inside the car. "Yes. It was beautiful. I can't thank you enough," I said. It really had been so special to me. After dropping Dee Dee off, we pulled up in front of my parents' home. Gino put the car in park and turned his head towards me. He had that little grin of his growing across his face. "You know, I really had a wonderful time with you tonight," he said the words to me so softly. "So did I," I said and in the pit of my stomach I felt butterflies again. My thoughts were racing through my mind. *Was he going to kiss me now? Was he going to make his move?* "So how would you feel if we made this a regular thing, you and me? Would you like that?" he asked. "Yeah I would," I said and smiled. *Ok, this is it. He's going to kiss me now.* I leaned in a little bit closer. I figured I would make it easier for him to make his move. He made a move, but it wasn't what I expected. He reached into his pocket and pulled out a satin pouch decorated with a Chinese motif and fastened with a snap button. "I picked up a little something special for you. It's your birthday gift. Here," he said and placed the small package in the palm of my hand. "You've done so much for me already. I can't accept this," I said. "Accept it. I'll be insulted if you don't. Besides, how can you turn something down before seeing it!" he said. I opened the pouch and couldn't believe my eyes. The pouch had two sections. In the first section, I slowly withdrew a delicate gold chain with a cross set in a gold nugget. In the other section of the pouch was a gold Longines watch with a little brown tiger face. I'd never seen anything like these gifts before. Later, I learned that the Mob had their own jewelers who created anything their hearts desired. I was stunned and sat their silently. "What's wrong? You don't like them? We can take them back and get others," he said as if concerned. "No I love them. I just never owned anything so beautiful," I said as I stared at the glittering gold pieces. "I have one other gift for you," he said and reached into his jacket pocket. I half expected him to pull out a magic wand but he had a wad of cash. "Here's a little something else for you to buy yourself and your daughter something nice," and he placed the cash in my hand. "Gino, I can't," before I could finish my sentence he cut me off. "Don't hesitate. Please don't. Now you and I have to say goodnight. I'm trying to keep myself under control. I'm a gentleman. Do you want me to walk you to your door?" he asked. "No, I'll be fine," I said overwhelmed by everything this amazing man had done for me in the course of one night. "Good night Joie. Sweet dreams," he said. I got out of the car and walked to my front door like I was walking on clouds. I was conscious of his eyes on me the whole way. As I closed the front door behind me, I heard his car pull off.

In the quiet of the living room, I found my mother sitting on the couch. She stood up to wait for me. "How was your date dear? Did you enjoy yourself?" she asked. "Ma, you're not going to believe this!" I said. I handed her the pouch. As she opened it up her eyes grew wide. "Oh my god! JoAnn, these are gorgeous! I can't believe this!" she said and pulled out the jewelry. She inspected each piece. "These are real gold!" she squealed. "Ma, that's not all he gave me," I said. "There's more?" she said with excitement. I took the wad of cash out of my clutch purse and handed it to her. She took it reluctantly and counted it. "JoAnn, there's five hundred dollars here!" I knew Gino gave me a lot but I almost fainted when she said how much it was. "He was the perfect gentleman Ma. He never even tried to kiss me once," I said. Saying out loud that Gino never kissed me left me feeling a little odd but also a bit confused as to why he didn't try. I brushed the thought off and chalked it up to him trying to be a gentleman. "Oh JoAnn, I'm so happy for you," she said. I was happy for me too. I felt like a little girl finding her fairy tale prince.

Gino and I went out several times after my birthday. Each date was a repeat of the first. It was always a whirlwind of extravagance that ended with gifts and cash. One night as we sat in his car he told me he was going on a business trip for a few days. He promised to take me out to dinner as soon as he returned. "Where would you like to go for our next date? Paris? New York? Milan? Let me know and we'll go." I just laughed it off. "You're crazy, you know that?" I said. "I'm serious Joie. You take your time and think about where you want to go for our next date and I'll have the Lear jet ready. I can fly you around the world" "Oh yeah? Well, where's it at?" I asked the question half jokingly and half truly curious. "It's parked at the airfield on 36th Street and got a tank of gas just waiting on you!" he said as if proud to be my world trip escort. I found out later he had access to the jet that the Mafia used to fly goods and people back and forth between Miami and Panama. "How about for now we stay on land. I think I'd rather have lunch in Miami with my little girl than fly to Paris." "Okay then. When I get back, we'll have lunch and take little Nikki out shopping. By the way Joie, I been meaning to ask you something. What's your favorite color?" I chuckled. This was the big question he's been *meaning to ask* me? "It's silver," I replied. It was so cute how he seemed inquisitive and genuinely interested in me. "I like that color. It's simple and goes with everything," he said. I laughed at how he said it so matter-of-factly. "I like artichokes too since you wanna know about me," and had a smile on my face. "Good to know," he said. Shortly afterwards we said our goodbyes. Gino always left me feeling so light on my feet like I was in the clouds.

Early the next morning, there was a knock on my front door. My father was home and the children all knew better then to wake him up. He was a pure bastard on a daily basis but wake him early and he would take bastard to another level! My mother attempted to get to the door before he did. She was a minute too late. My father swung the door open and looked directly at a delivery boy. "Hello. Good Morning sir. I have a delivery for a Miss JoAnn," the man said. The poor man had no idea what type of demon was standing in front of him. "What the fuck is it?" my father replied. The delivery boy looked a little shocked. "I'm sorry. It's right here," he said as he bent down and picked up a wicker basket full of artichokes. "Is this some kind of joke?" my father asked. "No sir. I was told to deliver to this address. All I need is your signature," he said as he put his hand out to show the paperwork of the delivery. My father snatched it from him and handed it to my mother. "Now you listen to me, I ain't paying for nothing I didn't order!" he grumbled. "Oh no sir, it has already been paid for," the delivery boy said. My mother scanned over the paperwork and wrote her signature at the bottom. "Here you are sir," she said and handed it all back to him. "Thank you, Ma'am," he said. I think it was out of a mix of being courteous and grateful that he could get the hell out of there. "I'll take that," she said and took the basket to the kitchen. "Have a nice day," he said and turned to go back to his truck. My father stood there and watched him get in his truck. He slammed the front door so hard we heard it through the whole house. "JoAnn! Get your ass down here!" he shouted. My mother came from the kitchen. "It was just a delivery Joseph. Please. It's too early," she begged. I was at the top of the stairs looking at them. In the pit of my stomach I felt a little sick because I knew his wrath was about to unleash. "Get the fuck down here!" he bellowed. Slowly I descended the stairs. I knew better then to open my mouth. "Joseph, it was just a gift. Please don't do this!" my mother pleaded with him. "Shut the fuck up bitch. No one is talking to you," he said. My mother went silent and put her head down.

Looking at my father as I reached the bottom of the stairs, he looked like a rattle snake ready to strike his prey. "Who the fuck is this man sending you things to my mother fucking house?" his question was more like an interrogation. "His name is Gino," softly I replied. I didn't want to invoke any more anger from him. "Gino? And where did you meet him at a whore house? No man I know goes out and buys all these presents and gives a bitch money the way he does after just meeting her," he said. It took everything in my power to stop myself from telling him he didn't know of any real men that's why. "Are you fucking him?" he demanded an answer. "No! I haven't even kissed him!" I replied. I felt like I was professing my innocence in front of an executioner. "Lies!" he shouted and slapped me. "You're a lying whore!" he said and slapped me again. Not a drop of tears fell from me. I looked him in the face with our eyes locked on each other and said "I'm not lying!" I had my hand to my face rubbing where he had smacked to slow down the stinging sensation but I still did not let a single tear form. "You ain't seeing him anymore!" he shouted. "That's it! I'm putting an end to this bullshit," he looked at me as if that really was going to be the end of it. "You're not messing this up for me," came out of my mouth so calm and simply. "I won't let you take the small bit of happiness from my life because you're miserable," the words were coming from me as if I was possessed. He became furious. "What did you say?" he asked as if *daring me* to say it again. I took his bait. "*I said* you're not messing this up for me. I'm going to keep seeing him and you're *not* going to stop me." My mother's eye grew wide and she backed up a little bit. She knew the type of rage that my father had and tried to interject. "JoAnn, please don't," she said with such sorrow. "Shut up bitch!" my father scolded her. "This is between me and her," and he looked me square in the eyes. "You're not seeing him anymore and if I hear you are, I'll kill you," and with that said he grabbed me by my hair and pulled me closer to him so my face was inches from his. "Do I make myself clear?" I just looked at him. I didn't say a word. "*I said* do I make myself clear?" his hand was still wrapped up in the long blonde tresses of my hair. Silence was all that was heard. He threw me to the floor and began striking me. With each blow growing harder than the next, I would not allow a sound to come from my body. Each hit intensified the anger and disdain inside of me towards him. Each second I endured his abuse further solidified how I had to escape. He beat me until he grew tired. My mother just stood by and watched in horror with tears streaming down her face. Once he realized I was not going to give him the satisfaction of hearing my cries he stopped. I laid on the floor curled up in the fetal position. The only sounds I could hear were from my daughter crying upstairs for her Mommy. My mother must have heard them too because she went to check on Nikki. He stood above me like an animal over a fresh kill. Both of us were catching our breath. Though I may have been wounded, I refused to let him see it. I refused to let him take my dignity.

With every ounce of my strength I pushed myself up from the floor and brushed off my clothes as if I merely stumbled and fell. I fixed my hair in front of him to demonstrate he may have hurt my body but my soul was still strong. He just looked on as he was still panting from the beating he dished out. I stepped towards the stairs and looked up to see my brother and sisters watching. Each step I ascended, I could feel pain shooting through my insides but I merely took a deep breath and slowly proceeded up. My siblings looked on as if viewing a gladiator stepping out from the ring. My father just observed from the bottom of the stairs as I rose up as if victorious. I had come to a point where my outer vessel of a body would get bruised but my spirit inside refused to be broken. Nikki was my reason to go on. She gave me the will to force myself. She was the living breath that gave life to me every day no matter what I went through.

As I reached the top of the stairs, my brother and sisters moved out of my way like a parting sea. I walked down the hallway with every bit of might left inside of me. Coming to my bedroom, I looked in upon my mother cradling Nikki in her arms. She rocked her to soothe the worries my child had for me. I held my arms out and she almost reluctantly gave Nikki to me. The look on my Mom's face was of true grief. "As a mother," she said "your job is to love and protect your children. Every day I fail you. How can I protect you from him, when I can't protect myself? Forgive me JoAnn." My eyes were upon my baby girl. Her angelic face was my salvation from the misery. My mother put her hands on my shoulders and gave my daughter a kiss on her cheek. She rose from the bed with her head down as if she herself was defeated. Quietly leaving the room, she shut the door behind her. The house was silent except for the sound of the television from downstairs. I sat on the edge of my bed cradling my child. All I could do in that moment was sing to my daughter. Eventually she drifted to sleep. After placing her in the crib, I went to run a bath to soak my body in warm water and ease the pain. I looked in the mirror at the bruises left behind and vowed to myself to not let defeat be my only option. Both myself and my child deserved better.

Several days later while at home getting ready for my shift at the restaurant I heard the phone ringing in the kitchen. "JoAnn, it's for you," my mother's voice called from the bottom of the stairs. "Who is it Ma?" I asked as I was still getting dressed. She never replied. She was too busy in the kitchen getting dinner ready for the night's meal. I hurried down the steps and picked up the phone. "Hello?" "Hey Joie. It's me Gino. You missed me?" I was never happier to hear his voice. "Of course I did. How have you been?" I asked. "I'm good. I'm back in town. I want to see you tonight," he said. Part of me was anxious to see him and part of me was embarrassed. I didn't want him to see the damage left behind from my father. "Tonight's not a good time. I got to work." I said hoping it would be enough for him to be discouraged. "So what. I'll come by there and see you." "No. No. It's ok. We can get together another night," I was desperately trying to get him to change his mind. I even threw in some suggestions of meeting up in a couple of days. "You trying to blow me off?" he said defensively. "No Gino. It's not that. I'm just, I'm busy. I promise another night will be better and we can get together. I got to go now. I'm going to be late for work." I hung the phone up. I really did have to make it to my shift but I also didn't want to give him the chance for rebuttal. I felt horrible treating Gino like that after all he had done for me. I had to fight myself from calling him back.

Later that evening while serving a table of a couple on a date, I looked up to see Gino entering the restaurant. I rushed through taking the order from the table and quickly went towards the back area where the soda fountain was. Dee Dee was standing back there fixing some drinks. "Dee Dee do me a favor," I asked her. "Sure what is it Joie?" curiously she replied. "Go out there and finish my table. I don't want Gino to see me." "Why? Something happen between you two? Is *he* who gave you the bruises?" she asked. Somewhat shocked from her point blank question I told her the truth. "No. He didn't give these to me. My father did. I don't want him to see me like this." I was at her mercy. I could see the pity in her eyes. "Ok Joie. I'll do it. Give me their check." She took over the table and didn't miss a step while I cowardly hid behind the soda fountain. I could hear footsteps coming up from behind me. "Did you drop something?" a familiar voice asked. It was Gino. Dee Dee gave away my location. She never could hold water. I knew I couldn't hide any longer. "No. I didn't lose anything." "So you're hiding from me then? Did I do something wrong?" he asked. He seemed truly perplexed. I lifted my head and let him look at me. The bruise on my cheek and busted lip were visible no matter how much make up I put on to hide them. "Who did this to you?" he demanded. I was scared to speak. "Joie, who did this to you? Tell me now," he said more as an order than an inquisition. "My father did while you were out of town. He doesn't want me to see you anymore. He said if I do, he'll kill me." From the moment we met, I had never seen rage flash in Gino's eyes until then. His face grew stern. "You're coming with me!" He took my arm and led me towards the door. "Gino, I'm working right now." "I said you're coming with me," he said and held tightly on to my arm. Dee Dee looked on from the side of a table she was serving. She was puzzled by what was happening. He led me straight out the front door of the diner and outside to the street. I was looking for his car and didn't see it. "Where's your car?" I asked. "I don't have it. We're taking your car." "Gino, I don't have a car. I take the bus." I felt so pathetic saying that to him. He led me to a silver Cadillac. "Get in." "What the hell?" I was confused. "Gino this isn't my car. I can't get in this." "This *is* your car. Now get in it!" he said it so strongly I followed his instructions. "Are you telling me you got me a car?" "Yeah. It was your surprise. I had been planning it since before I left." "Where are we going?" I asked. "Your house. Your father and I are going to have some words." Gino and my father had never met. I never wanted him to be subjected to the reality of my life. I didn't want him to feel sorry for me either. Pulling up outside of my house, I could see the lights to the living room were on which meant my father was probably drunk in front of the television. Gino put the car in park. "Go inside and tell your father I want to meet him," he said. "Gino, I'm not sure about this." "I don't care what you're sure about just do it," he looked at me more like a parental figure in that moment. I opened the door to the Cadillac and went up the stairs. Stepping through the front door I found exactly what I knew I would, my father was drunk and in front of the television watching *"All in the Family."* It was ironic to me how he could watch all these images of families that love each other but was a pure demon to his own. He looked at me as I entered the room. "What the fuck are you doing home? Aren't you supposed to be working?" he asked. "My friend Gino wants to meet you." "Yeah, who's that?" "He's the guy that sent me the basket of artichokes." His interest peaked. "Oh yeah, well you tell your friend I'm in an important meeting right now and I'm not available." He always found a way to be a complete asshole but the extra touch of sarcasm really put him over the top. "He's outside. He said he wants to meet with you." "*And I said* I'm fucking busy," he roared. "Well, he's outside waiting to speak with you," I told him. My father pushed himself up from the chair. He was a tall man and built solid despite his lack of physical activities. Before I knew it he smacked me. I stood there with my hands covering my face. "What the fuck is wrong with you? You come in to my mother fucking house and demand I meet someone. Did you forget who the fuck I am?" he yelled. My mother came rushing into the room to see what was going on. My father raised his arm again to strike me. That's when Gino grabbed his arm. "She knows who you are," he said. My father was surprised that his grip was so strong on him. "Who the fuck are you?" he said to Gino. Every word he spoke left the smell of Jack Daniels trailing behind. "I'm Gino and I want to talk to you. We can do this the easy way like two gentlemen or we can do this the hard way. Believe me, the hard way is not an option you really want to choose." Uncertain about the situation, my father looked around the room at me and my mom. "The easy way," he replied. Gino let go of his arm. "Now is there a place we can go sit and talk," Gino asked. He was calm as if nothing just happened between the two. Gino was a man who spoke softly but always had the air of power around him. They went to the dining room and sat at the table. My mother and I sat within listening distance on the couch. My father lit a cigarette not really to smoke it but to make him feel more grounded. Then he took out his flask and took a couple sips from it. He offered Gino some but he turned it down. "I don't drink," he said to my father. I knew it was a lie. "I don't trust a man that doesn't drink," he said to Gino. Gino simply brushed it off. "I'm an honorable man, Mr. Spondike," Gino said amicably. Gino reached into his breast pocket and pulled out a pack of cigarettes. He calmly lit it and pulled a drag. It seemed as though he was giving him the chance to calm down and sober up a bit. "Mr. Spondike, you seem like a hardworking man. You seem to like the type that goes out every day to earn a decent paycheck. I know at times things can be difficult for you. That is why I have a proposal for you." My mother and I just looked at each other and bit our tongues. My father was many things but a hardworking man he wasn't. We knew Gino was trying to butter him up. "It must be overwhelming to you to keep a roof over your family's head and feed them. A wife, kids, and a grandchild. So I sit here before you to make a bit of an offer to lighten your load. I'm going to be honest with you. I've only known your daughter for a little while now but I want to take her, and of course her child, off your hands. I want to provide them a better life. A whole new lifestyle that you wouldn't be able to provide. This will help you in return. A couple less mouths to feed," Gino made his offer to my father and took a drag off of his cigarette to let his words sink in. My mother and I were in shock we couldn't believe what he just said. Gino and I only knew each other for a few weeks and he planned to whisk me and my daughter away from everything we knew. "You want me to let you take them?" My father let out a little chuckle. "You want the bitch and her kid then take them," he took a sip off of his flask. My mother got up from the couch and burst into their meeting. "You're just going to give your family away. Just like that. Do you even care about us at all?" she was overloaded with emotions. "Mrs. Spondike, I assure you your family will be well provided for," Gino said as comforting as he could. My mother has been all for my relationship with Gino but didn't like the idea of just handing me and my daughter over to him like we were cattle for him to raise. "This isn't right," she said. I stepped in to the dining room. "You want to go with this man?" my father asked. All eyes fell upon me. I didn't truthfully know who Gino was. We had only been dating a few short weeks. I didn't really know what his lifestyle truly was about there had only been guessing games between myself and Dee Dee. In that instant everything inside of me said this was my way out. My sister's voice and words kept playing in my head. This was my escape from the nightmare I called my life. This was mine and my child's ticket to freedom. I hesitated for a moment because of the look on my mother's face. "Yes. Yes, I want to go with him," I replied. My mother left the room sobbing. "It's settled then," Gino said to my father. "She and her child leave with me tonight." Gino looked at me and told me to get my daughter. "I have a few things I want to take. I will go gather them up," and with that I turned and left the dining room.

As I was going up the stairs I realized I was leaving my siblings behind. There would be no one to protect them from the Beast anymore. I peaked in to their bedroom and watched as they slept peacefully in the bed. I didn't want to wake them up. I knew it would be better and easier for me to leave without them having the chance to beg me to stay. Besides being a sister, I knew I was a mother now. I had to make the best choice for my daughter. Leaving the abuse of my father was definitely the best thing for her. I walked up the hallway to my room. I heard my mother softly crying. Entering the room, I saw Nikki asleep in her crib. All my love was wrapped up in this adorable child christened as Nicole Lyn Levy. "What are you doing JoAnn? You don't even know this man!" she said. It was her feeble attempt to beg me to stay. "Ma, anything is better than staying here. I can't let Nikki live like this," I said to her in a Mother – to – Mother manner. "You're right. Anything is better here," she said as she wiped away the tears that had drenched her face. "Let me help you pack," she said as her way of showing she supported me. "Just pack Nikki's clothes. I grab what I want of mine."

Truthfully, I didn't have much to pack up. There was the bottle of perfume and jewelry Gino had given me, some photos, clothes and a few pairs of shoes. In the end both mine and my daughter's lives with my family were able to fit in two suitcases and a small duffle bag.

Coming down the stairs with the luggage and my mother following close behind with Nikki in her arms we saw Gino standing in front of the door waiting. He took the luggage from me and brought it out to the car. My father was back in his usual spot by the television. He didn't attempt to get up and say any goodbyes and I didn't expect him to. Who really expects the Devil to give best wishes to someone? My mother held Nikki close to her. She gave her a kiss on the forehead and handed her over to me. Gino came back quickly. "Are we ready to go?" he asked. "Yeah. I think we are." I looked at my mother. "I love you Ma." "I love you too Joie. Take good care of them," she said to Gino. "I give you my word Mrs. Spondike," Gino said and opened the door for me to carry little Nikki to the car. In that moment, I stepped out of my family's home and knew it would be forever. I felt disoriented. I had no idea what to expect but I still breathed a small sigh of relief knowing the torture of my father had come to an end.

## Chapter Four:  Lifestyles of the Rich and Nameless

As the car came to a slow stop, I noticed we were parked in front of a small condominium complex in the Miami Shores area.  It was dark but I could see the trees were trimmed perfectly.  No one was outside in the neighborhood.  The only sounds to be heard were the passing cars and chirps from the crickets hiding in bushes.  It was a vast comparison to where I lived with my family.  It was almost bizarre to me to experience the peacefulness.  My eyes kept darting around taking in my surroundings.  "Where are we?" I asked while still holding Nikki in my arms since we left my parents home.  "We're at my place. *Our place*," Gino said.  I could tell he was a little apprehensive with the situation as well.  In a way, it helped me to settle down a bit seeing he felt the same way.  Gino grabbed the bags from the trunk of the car.  "Ok. Follow me," he said as he led the way to a small staircase.  Gino's apartment was on the second floor of the three story apartment building.  As he put the key in to the lock, I began to imagine what was on the other side of the door.  I knew a little bit about his lifestyle so I was half expecting guns and rocket launchers to be on the tables.  As he held the door open for me and Nikki, I found myself surprised with what I saw. It was a moderate sized two bedroom set up. The interior was decorated in what appeared to be traditional Italian style; greens, reds, golds and oranges filled the living room with color. Religious statues were scattered throughout the places. Paintings and photographs lined the walls. For a bachelor, his home was very clean and inviting.

Gino placed the luggage in what appeared to be his guest room. "Here's your room. Make yourself at home. There's not much food in the fridge right now. I have some shopping to do. Make a list of foods you and Nikki like and I'll have someone get them. If there's anything else you need don't hesitate to let me know. The world is at your fingertips now Joie." Gino may have been feared by many but to those whom he chose to open up to he was a very loving man. "Nikki can sleep with me tonight in the bed but I really should have brought her crib. Maybe I can go and get it in the morning from my parents' home," I said. "I'll buy her another one. The best one in any color you want. I'll make sure she gets put in a good day care or if you prefer her to have a Nanny I'll find one. She will be well provided for." I wasn't used to anyone but my Mother caring for Nikki so the idea of having to place her in daycare or with a nanny was something I hadn't realized I would need to consider. Gino may not have been Nikki's biological father but he showed her love as if she was his own. "Try to get some rest. We got a big day tomorrow," he said. "What's tomorrow?" I was curious if there was something else I needed to brace myself for. A lot had changed within just a few hours for me and Nikki. "We're going shopping. We're going to make sure you and Nikki have everything you need," he said. "Gino, I don't know how to repay you for all of this," I said. I couldn't believe how a man who barely knew me and my daughter could show so much love and concern. "There's no need to repay me," he said softly and left the bedroom shutting the door behind him. I laid on the bed that night with my daughter nestled next to me on the bed and pillows going over the day's events. Thoughts were racing through my mind on how my life just made a major change in paths and I had no clue what was next to come but I did know I couldn't turn back now.

The next morning I woke up to find fresh flowers on the dresser. They were a beautiful mixture of some of Florida's wild flowers arranged perfectly in a crystal vase. Sitting next to them was a tray of with bagels and cream cheese, muffins, and a pitcher of some fresh squeezed orange juice. There was a note that read, "Be back soon. *Mangiare e divertirsi!*" I found out later it was the Italian way of saying "*eat and enjoy.*" Nikki was still asleep so I took the opportunity to relish in the bounty that was left for me. I wasn't really used to eating breakfast. My mother never really prepared it. There were many days my siblings and I didn't eat lunch either. We just became accustomed to going without and making the best of things. After my meal, I decided to take a hot shower to jump start my day.

Turning the water off to the shower, I heard the familiar sounds of Nikki stirring from her slumber. I truly saw my daughter as the only source of pure love in my life. I laid next to her on the bed in my towel and played with her little toes. Her laughter was like music to me. Getting Nikki dressed for the day was so much fun for me. I adored styling up her blonde curly locks of hair in pretty bows and barrettes. From the money Gino gave me for my birthday, I had bought her a cute pink dress with lace and ruffles with a matching pair of white sandals embroidered with little pink roses. By the time she was ready for the day, she looked like a real life baby doll. The best part was- she was all mine. From the bedroom, I heard the entrance door open and the sounds of footsteps. I poked my head out and saw Gino. He had finally come back and was dressed in a pair of khaki slacks and a button down shirt. His usual jewelry dripping from his neck and wrists. He looked happy to see me, like a husband coming home to his wife. "Hello there. Did you enjoy your breakfast?" he asked with a smile on his face. "I did and the flowers are beautiful." "It's nothing. I just wanted you and Nikki to wake up to something nice," he said dismissively. "So you ladies ready to go shopping?" he asked. "Yeah, Nikki is all dressed." "Good we can take your car," he said. It still really didn't hit me that this man went out and bought a brand new Cadillac for me in my favorite color none-the-less. I couldn't help but chuckle. "Gino, what made you buy me a car?" "I felt you didn't have one so why not?" he said playfully. "Now come on let's go," with excitement in his voice he scooped Nikki up and we were out the door to hit a strip of stores in downtown Miami I never would have dared to shop in before.

The sky was a perfect blend of blues and there was breeze sweeping in from the water and filtering through the haze of Miami's downtown pollution. It was as if it was a sign from nature saying today is a new beginning. Gino and I took Nikki for a brief lunch at a little café on the strip. Everything felt so new. Even the food I ate that day tasted better. After lunch, we began to shop which was something Gino loved to do more than me. Our first stop was at Burdines. Stepping inside the department store that day truly was the first insight as to what was to come for me and Nikki. Gino noticed me looking around at the clothes on the racks, the jewelry counter, the perfumes and the Lancôme counter. Gino looked at me and said, "Joie. Pick out whatever you want. Money is not a concern." He took my hand and led me over to a sales girl. "Hi, how are you both today?" she said. She had a warm and inviting smile. She was wearing a black skirt and blazer with a white satin blouse for contrast. Her hair was pulled back in a Jackie Onassis style. I noticed she was wearing a set of pearl earrings to bring the whole look together. She looked flawless and classy. She looked like someone who had their life well put together. "Listen, I'm with her and she's with me," Gino said. He pulled out a thick wad of cash and took out a couple hundred dollars. He placed them in her hand. "Give her whatever she wants. Don't leave her side until she is done." She saleswoman smiled at Gino and said, "She's in very good hands sir. It will be my pleasure to assist you both today." She led me to the counter and that's when the fun started. "Ok sweetie, let me take a good look at you." She sat me down at the counter and brought out all kinds of products, expensive products; blush, mascara, eye-liner, lip-liner, eyebrow pencils and more. By the time she got done with my make over I looked like a totally different woman and felt like it too. Gino was grinning from ear to ear. "What a knock out!" he said. The saleswoman, whose name I learned was Kate by the time my makeover was completed, led me to the perfume counter next. The bottles glistened like diamonds. Each fragrance smelled more beautiful and delicate than the last. I was actually having fun spraying each one to figure out which I liked best.

Gino said in his typical fashion, "If you can't decide, just take one of each." By the time Kate and I were through I left that area with bags filled with over four hundred dollars worth of products and a whole new confidence about myself. Heading towards the escalator Gino spotted a familiar face, it was Tommy Russo. Tommy Russo looked like your typical Italian-American with his short dark hair and standard build. He was a part of the Mafia with Gino. Tommy's role was a low level runner or an errand boy and never really rose any higher in the ranks. Tommy and Gino greeted each other as they walked passed one another. There was a mutual respect among them. By Tommy's side was a young woman with clothes too tight and tits too high to match the heels on her feet. She was pale in comparison to the saleswoman I had just left. There was nothing classy about her. Gino filled me in on her. Her name was Marge and she was one of Tommy's mistresses. Tommy was married with quite a few extra ladies on the side but this one was his favorite. Gino told me Marge didn't do anything for Tommy not even sleep with him. Rarely did they spend time together but he still bought her everything her heart desired. Following closely behind them was a store associate pushing an entire clothing rack. Gino said Tommy's girl usually liked to shop until two racks were filled. Apparently that day was a light shopping spree for them.

Stepping off the escalator, my eyes targeted a sweater on a mannequin that was placed on a high shelf. Gino spotted me staring. He quickly found a saleswoman and said, "Give her that sweater." "Sir, that's a display. I would be more than happy to find one from the rack for her," the woman said. "Give her that one!" he said and placed a hundred dollar bill in the breast pocket of her silk blouse. "Of course sir," the woman nodded her head and was quickly on her way to find a ladder. I just stood there with a smirk. Gino knew how to get things done and I admired that about him. Soon the woman brought the sweater to me. I was almost too afraid to touch the beautiful cashmere. I looked at the tag and it read "Made in Italy." Then I saw the price. It was fifteen hundred dollars. "Oh my God, that's a lot of money!" I said. Gino waved his hand dismissively. "What do you expect? Its Italian made. You like it don't you?" he asked. "Of course I do, Gino." "Then get some matching slacks for it," he said assuring me he had it covered. I looked at the saleswoman. "I guess you have to show me where to find those then," I said in a matter-of-fact way. "Of course ma'am," she said. "Before you do that, go get three racks. We have a lot of shopping to do," Gino said. The saleswoman and I looked puzzled at him. "I'm not gonna be out done by Tommy," he said and winked at me. I couldn't help but burst out laughing. The saleswoman was clueless but followed Gino's instructions. She soon returned with the racks and we were on our way. Row after row of beautiful clothes, we went through and picked out what I thought were breathtaking ensembles. I loved the materials, the colors, the patterns. Silk. Satin. Lace. Cashmere. One expensive tag after another. Gino just stood back and let me find my buried treasures without batting an eyelash. I felt like the First Lady with my own personal assistant following closely behind me. Gino was like my President, a man of power and prestige. The entire day was spent with him giving the orders of go-ahead and people would follow his direction. The common thread of his instruction was simple. "Give her what she wants and keep her happy." I was happy. I was thrilled. What woman *wouldn't* love to walk in to a department store and grab whatever she wanted without even worrying about the prices? Gino truly was spoiling me and I wasn't complaining. As we came towards the end of the women's department I spotted the children's area. Nikki had been so well behaved that day. Gino felt she deserved to be spoiled to. Anyone could see he fell in love with my daughter. Nikki spotted a stuffed teddy bear and grabbed it like a pro. She gave it a big hug and was delighted to hear music come from its chubby body. The sweet melody was so thrilling to her. Gino let her keep it. He told me to get her some outfits, shoes and whatever other toys she wanted. I loved shopping for myself but shopping for my daughter was even more exciting and fulfilling. After several hours of shopping and thousands of dollars later we were finally ready to head home. The first day of my new life was coming to a close and left a taste in my mouth that I enjoyed and savored. It was highly addictive and I was already hooked.

**Joie Miami**

**Chapter Five:  For Better or Worse**

It didn't take long for Gino and I to find a daily routine together. We found comfort in each other's presence.  Every morning he'd get up early with me for a cup of coffee and breakfast.  Afterwards, I would get Nikki ready for her day and place her on the school bus.  Gino would soon be on his way as well.  While Gino disappeared for several hours out of each day, I would find things to do to fill my time.  I still kept my employment at the diner for a while.  It wasn't that I really needed the money because Gino ensured I had everything I ever dreamed of.  I kept my job to still feel as though I was on my own two feet.  Plus, the money I made was put aside in a bank account for rainy days or just in case Gino ever grew tired of me and Nikki being around.  On my days off, I would visit with my mother when my father wasn't around.  This went on for months.  On the surface we were a normal functioning family but as the saying goes, *"Never judge a book by its cover."*

In the months that went by, never once did Gino and I have sex. There was never a kiss between us either.  I knew it was unusual for a man and woman to live together like husband and wife and not share any intimacy. Gino did a lot for me and never asked for anything in return. One night I sat and thought about how my life had changed. I began to wonder why a man would take me away from an abusive situation and buy lavish things for me and my child and not want something in return. I learned at a young age all men are out for something. With so many questions beginning to build in my mind, I worked up the courage to finally ask Gino what was really going on.

Returning from another day of what Gino considered "work" he greeted me and then headed towards his bedroom to change clothes. I followed closely behind him. "Gino, can we talk?" I asked. He looked a little curious since I had never ventured on to his side of our domain before. "Sure doll. Have a seat," he said and gestured to the bed. I took a moment to find the right words. "Gino, what is this? What is going on between us?" I asked. It felt good to get them out in to the open. "What do you mean?" he asked. "I mean this- you and me. We live together on a daily basis. You take me on shopping sprees. You buy things for my child and get her put in to a private nursery. You take care of everything for us but don't ask for anything. Why? Why are you doing this for me? What do you want out of all of this?" Gino looked at me like he was trying to figure out how to answer my questions. "I'm doing this for you Joie because I see you're a good woman who had a bad deal. I saw you trying to do your best for your child even through the shit you had to deal with. You're a fighter Joie. You don't fold easily. People like that are hard to come by." It took a moment for me to digest what he had said but I still had more questions and wanted answers. "What am I to you? Am I your room mate or your lady? We haven't even kissed or made love? Do I turn you on?" Gino just smiled at me. "Joie who *wouldn't* be attracted to you? You're a knock out." "So what's going on Gino? You leave all day and don't tell me where you're going. Is there someone else?" The words came out of my mouth like bullets but I didn't care. Gino realized in that moment I wasn't going to cave. He knew I was a woman that had a strong will and wouldn't take any more excuses. "Listen Joie, your daughter is very young. This is all new and different for her. She's away from everything she was used to and it must be complicated for her to understand the changes. I'm trying to wait until she adjusts better. I'm a gentleman who has respect for you. I'm not some young punk just trying to get in to your pants. I'm not like that. I want you to know when the time is right we can work on things between us but it's just not the right time. No Joie, there's no other woman. We are in this together, you and me, for better or worse." Gino's words were so tender. The look in his eyes told me he was telling the truth. "Why are you gone all day Gino without telling me where you're going? Who are you with?" I wanted the truth and I didn't care how bad it was. I knew the rumors. I seen the kind of money he went around flashing. There was nothing that would rattle me or horrify me. I simply wanted the truth. Gino took my hand in his and raised it to his lips. He kissed it softly. "For better or worse," he said. I knew then I wasn't going to get much from him. His secrets were under lock and I didn't have the key just yet.

After my night of playing an unsuccessful game of "20 Questions" with Gino I knew the only way to find out the answers I was looking for was to have a strategy. My best plan was to be quiet and observe. I began to pay better attention to my surroundings, the people that came and went and the vehicles. Any kind of clue that would give me some insight to the real world Gino was from I would exam closely. My biggest tip off came one day when there was a knock on our apartment door. I was tending to dinner and Nikki so Gino went to answer it. When the door opened up I heard a man's voice. I poked my head slightly out from the kitchen entrance and spotted a familiar face. It was Tommy Russo. I remembered his face from our shopping spree. I heard him tell Gino there was a call from "The Old Man." Without hesitation, Gino went with Tommy. Ten minutes later he came back as if nothing happened. "Who was it Gino?" I asked from the kitchen. I took the chance to play a little clueless to see if I could get something out of him.

"What do you mean?" he asked. "Who was at the door?" I made it seem as though I hadn't seen Tommy's face. "Oh. It was Tommy. He had a call for me next door," he answered. "Next door? Tommy's our neighbor?" I was actually shocked. I had never seen anyone come and go from the apartment across the hall since Nikki and I arrived. I actually thought we were the only ones living on the floor. "Yeah he moved in a while ago. This building is old and sometimes the calls get crossed," he said. I think it was his way of trying to get my attention off of the call. I may have been young but I certainly wasn't stupid. I knew better then to believe phone calls would go to the wrong apartment but I let him play it off. I didn't want to stir the pot up too much.

Tommy's visit that night was the first of many. Each time he knocked on the door it was for the same reason- The Old Man was calling. Once I worked up the nerve to ask Gino who The Old Man was that called for him. Gino simply said it was his father. It actually struck me as funny because he rarely talked about his family. Still, I knew he was lying. I found out later The Old Man was really Hyman Larner, Gino's boss.

*Hyman Larner was a very powerful man associated with Sam Giancana and the Chicago Outfit of the Mafia. He was considered "Ivy League" among the usual gangsters. He was the Jewish brain behind the Italian muscle and had real connections through key players in the CIA and among world leaders. Larner was truly the man that expanded the Mafia and their game from slot machines and gambling to the smuggling operations and money laundering through Panama, Asia and the Arab nations.*

Gino never discussed the phone calls with me. He would always say he had to go away on "business" trips. Nothing more in details would be provided and nothing was ever questioned by me. I learned he was going to be tight lipped with me and I had grown accustomed to it. I also grew accustomed to him returning from these trips with lavish gifts of clothes and jewelry. He truly did spoil me in such a way where I started to expect nothing less. A hunger for more began to grow inside of me. I wanted to find a way to stay on Gino's good side and demonstrate to him that he could trust me. I wanted him to open up to me a bit. I knew it meant I would have to rely on my female charm.

Gino had been away on one of his business trips for a few days and was returning soon. While he was gone, it was business as usual for me and Nikki. I would drop her off at the daycare and take the rest of the day to run errands, visit with my mother and do some shopping. While out and about on one of my excursions, I spotted a jewelry store with a sign in the window that said "Engraving." It had given me a good idea for a gift to show my appreciation to Gino and all he had done for me and my daughter. It made me feel good to return some kindness. I finished my day with a trip to the market and picked up some items for dinner. I knew Gino loved my cooking.

At home, I had the pots going on the stove and wine already chilled. When Gino arrived I truly was excited to see him and seen the joy in his face. "Hey babe, what's cooking?" he asked. I knew it was a play on words and couldn't help but chuckle. "You're so silly. I got some pasta and salad for us to enjoy. There's a bottle of Pinot Noir in the fridge," I said. "Why don't you go and get cleaned up while I finish up here and get dinner ready?" "Okay babe. Where's Nikki?" Gino was always very observant and attached to my little girl. "I made arrangements for Nikki to spend the night with my mother to give you and me a chance at some private time." Gino looked up at me while he took off his shoes. He had a slight grin on his face that I came to realize was his signature. Gino went to his room to take a shower. While he was busy, I was working hard to make sure our dinner was special. I set the plates and glasses, poured the wine and lit the candles for the perfect setting.

Gino and I enjoyed dinner and each other's company. We truly did find comfort in one another despite our age difference. We talked and laughed that night. It was nice to have a moment together to bond. "Gino, I have something special I want to give you," I said. "Joie, you didn't have to get me anything," he said. "I know I didn't have to. I wanted to. So, do me a favor and open it up." I put a small black box on the table in front of him. Gino looked at the box with curiosity. "What's this?" he asked. "Open it and find out," I said. Gino took the box in his hand and gave it a little shake by his ear to tease me. The anticipation of him opening the box was his way of keeping things fun between us. "Okay, here goes. It's not gonna explode is it?" he asked jokingly. "Of course not! Gino open it up!" "Okay okay," he said and lifted the lid. Inside was a gold Figaro link chain with an oval shaped medallion I had engraved. The medallion read, *I'll love you for as long as I live and live for as long as I love you.*" Gino took it out of the box. "It's beautiful Joie. Thank you. This is the nicest thing I have gotten in a long time," he said. He took my hand in his and looked in my eyes. "I'm glad you like it," I said. "I love it," he replied. His eyes were locked on me. I leaned in closely and gave him a long awaited kiss on his lips. There was something special about that kiss. It made me feel like all was right in the world. In that moment it was as if everything and everyone else was off in the distance and all that existed was me and him. I could tell he felt it too. He reached over to embrace me and give me another kiss. It was done so passionately that I felt a wave of heat and tingling sensations wash over me. My body felt craving his touch.

Gino took my hand and led me to the long, brown leather couch. He sat next to me quietly for a second. It was as if he was collecting his thoughts. I touched his shoulder and smiled at him. Tonight was our night. It was the night we both had waited a very long time for. "Joie," he said my name almost in a whisper. "It's time Gino. I'm ready," I said to him. He put his arms around me and held me close to him. The strength of him was something I welcomed. He kissed my neck softly and I let out a gasp. My body felt on fire from my desires. "Come in to the room with me," he said and led again into his bedroom. He pulled down the bedspread and came back to my side. He stood in front of me. He seemed more nervous that I was. "God, you're so young," he said as his hands traveled up and down my body with his eyes following close behind. He caressed my breasts and leaned over to kiss them. He softly rubbed his face next to mine and stroked the long blonde tresses of my hair. "You're so beautiful," he said and kissed my lips. "I've waited a long time for this. I wanted you to know I respect you. I never wanted you to think that I wanted was just this. I've always wanted you Joie. I couldn't bring myself to make a move because I wanted the timing to be right. I wanted it to be perfect," he said. I could feel the truth in his words. "I've wanted you to Gino. I'm so happy we're together," I said to him. I took a step back and slowly took my clothes off while he watched. It was if his knees were a little weak because I could see him trying to hold steady. I stepped out of my small pile of clothes on the floor and kissed his lips again. Slowly I unbuttoned his shirt and kissed his chest making my way down to his belt. I may have been young but I definitely wasn't a virgin. I was able to open his belt with one hand and undo his pants with the other. Gino looked down at me and I smiled while I gently took his manhood in my hands and began to stroke it. He made a slight moan from the sensation and it excited me. It didn't take long before Gino to be at full attention and I enjoyed the view. I opened my mouth and took him inside. Gino was gasping for air. I knew Gino was not sleeping around on me so the interaction between us was the first we both felt in a very long time. I continued to please Gino to the point where he couldn't stand it anymore. He reached down and picked me up in his strong arms. He placed me on the bed and kissed all over my body. He was passionate and romantic. It felt so right when he entered my body. It felt natural. With each movement and motion of his body I felt ready to explode. We made love for several hours until we were both worn out. When we were done, we laid in bed together wrapped in the sheets and shared a cigarette. "Well did it feel okay? You know I'm the man," he said. We both laughed and were giddy from the moment we just shared. Gino was very good in bed. He was sensual and took his time in everything he did. He may have had three decades on me, but he wasn't old and decrepit. Actually, he was in phenomenal shape with flat abs and a tight ass to match. My Mother always teased me about his "nice buns." Gino's skin was soft and smooth too. All together Gino made for a sexy package, especially with his laid-back, cocky attitude. "In the morning we'll get Nikki and do some shopping," he said. He put his head on my shoulder. I finished up our cigarette. "In the morning. But right now it's still our time," I said and held his close. "It is. Isn't it," he said. I felt him kissing my neck. It didn't take long for us to get in to a second round that night. In the morning, just as he said, we got ready, picked up Nikki and went out to shop. It shortly became a pattern between us. Every time we had sex, he always felt he had to give me money or buy me something special. In those days, things just seemed to be so pristine between us until the veil that was over my eyes slowly was pulled back to reveal the truth.

Joie Miami

## Chapter Six: Eyes Wide Shut

In the days, weeks and months that slowly began to follow our first night of love making, I started to notice a slight change to Gino's personality. At first it was small gestures of jealousy but progressively it grew to a possessive nature. Soon, I wasn't able to freely move about to do my own shopping or small daily chores as before. Suddenly, I had to ask permission to things. When we would have conversations at night about things I needed for Nikki or myself and by the morning those items would appear. If I mentioned a certain lotion or soap I liked and wanted to go pick up the next day the bathroom cabinets would be stocked to the brim. If Nikki wanted a special cereal or juice, our kitchen would be flooded with bottles and boxes. Clothes shopping became a thing of the past. I would find boxes of clothes and shoes laid out on my bed with matching jewelry and purses. Gino even set me up with a personal tailor who made clothing for Joe DiMaggio as well.

It wasn't just the shopping and outings that changed. I had to quit my job at the restaurant which was disappointing because I liked earning my own money just in case something went down between Gino and me. I also knew I would miss Dee Dee. She was one of the only close female friends I had. Nikki was changed from the school she had grown accustomed to attending. She was enrolled into a private nursery which I later found out many of the other children of those involved in the Mafia went to. It was an easy way of ensuring her safety. Those she was allowed to have play dates with were hand selected by Gino as well, and it was a very small number. Even who I was allowed to interact with ended up being wives and girl friends of Gino's associates. I began to slowly realize that Gino may have saved me and my child from an abusive man but it came with a price. The feeling of being trapped became a reality. It was his way of keeping me hidden from his family and friends since we had such a large age gap between us. Gino may have treated me like a Queen but I had no power in the kingdom.

The "Princess in the tower" life grew very old very quickly. Six months had gone by and I was growing tired of it real fast. I needed excitement in my life. I needed a change. I may have had everything a girl could have wanted but I was still missing something and I knew it. Gino could tell that I was starting to get annoyed with the way things were. He began to spend time at home during the nights in the hopes that it would alleviate whatever I was going through but truthfully it made things worse. I needed human interaction with other people. I was still young and sitting at home watching television every night wasn't my idea of a good time. "Joie, what's wrong?" Gino asked one night while we sat next to each other eating dinner. "What do you mean?" I asked. "I can tell you're not happy. What's bothering you?" he asked. "What's bothering me? You really want to know. I'm stuck in this place all day and night. I have to ask for permission to go places and have no friends. I need some adult interaction. I want some fun for a change," I said. Gino looked at me carefully as if he was choosing his words wisely. "Fun. Okay, I can do that. Why don't we have a cocktail party? I can invite some people over and we can have drinks like adults do. Would that make you happy?" It was the first time he had ever said he would invite people over to meet me. Though it seemed like a small gesture it actually was a very big deal. "I would love to have people over. When can we do it?" I truly was excited and I wasn't about to let him change his mind. "How about Friday? That seems like a good day for me. Why don't you plan the whole thing? Whatever foods and drinks you want we can have. It'll be nice," he said. "Friday it is!" I said and couldn't help but smile. The thoughts of what foods and drinks I could serve entered my head. It was my first adult cocktail party so I wanted it to be just right.

Friday morning I wrote out a list of grocery items I would need to prepare the hors d'oeuvres. I even wrote down some wines and liquors I thought everyone would enjoy. Gino had everything delivered to me at the time I wanted them by and soon I was in the kitchen working hard. Gino came home a little early to check on me and see if I needed anything else. He was amused to see tray after tray of appetizers, wine and liquor bottles chilled and even desserts were being made. "Looks like you got all of this under control," he said. "I do. I hope everyone likes it. How many people are coming?" I asked. It struck me in that moment Gino never told me who he was inviting and I was making food for a small army. "I invited Tommy Russo, my friends Sonny and Vinnie and Sal and his wife Gracie." "Oh. I thought there was going to be more but there's plenty of food and drinks for everyone," I said as I stepped away to go and freshen up for the night's company.    There was a bounce to my step again, a bright twinkle in my eye and a certain glow of happiness that Gino noticed. After a quick shower I put lotion and perfume all over my body. I made sure my hair and makeup were perfect. I appraised myself in the smoked glass mirror as I crossed the living room to ensure I looked ready to take on the world. After all, these were not only Gino's friends but associates as well. "Baby you look so sexy," Gino said as he spotted me. "I'm almost ready to cancel tonight and take you right now." "Oh no you don't, not after all the work I've just gone through," I said with a smile and put my hands on my hips. An hour later there was a knock on the door and I couldn't help but be eager for my night to begin.

Tommy was the first to arrive since he lived right across the hall. I opened the door and introduced myself. Tommy handed me a bottle of champagne, it was in that moment that it struck me I had never seen his official wife. I wasn't about the drama and tonight was special so I didn't want to ask about her. I simply welcomed him in and told him where to find Gino. He went to greet Gino in the living room while I put the champagne on ice. A knock at the door soon came again, this time it was Sonny and Vinnie.

*Sonny was Sonny Pacini dubbed "Mr. Coffee" was tall handsome and I came to find out later to be very homosexual. He got his nickname for two reasons; he drank a shit load of coffee and had some extra sugar in his tank. Sonny was a runner from the Chicago crew. He would come and check out things from time to time in Miami just to make sure everything was running in top order. Sonny had a transvestite for a girlfriend named "Carmen." Sonny tried to play it off like she was a real woman but the Adam's apple was unmistakable. I do have to give it up to her because for a man she looked just like Sophia Loren. He would bring her around when he came in to town and surprisingly the others were very patient but they still loved to yank his chain about it. Vinnie ended up being Vincenzo Ruotolo another Mafia underling. He would do whatever job ordered to make a quick buck. He was someone who had a good spirit about him though. It was a shame that I was the one that ended up planning his mother and father's funerals.*

I opened the door and said hello. "Excuse me Miss. We must have the wrong place," Vinnie said. "Are you here for Gino?" I asked. "Yeah," said Sonny as he looked me up and down. "I'm Joie. Gino is in the living room. Please, come in." They came in and spotted Gino and Tommy in the living room. "Gino, that's quite a catch you got there," said Vinnie while he looked in my direction. "I'm a very lucky man," said Gino as he looked my way too. "Would anyone like some hors d'oeuvres? I made them all fresh," I said and placed out a few trays on the coffee table. As everyone began to help themselves I heard another knock on the door. Sal and Gracie had finally arrived. Gracie had a true air about her that seemed so familiar. It was a tough exterior similar to the one I had. She was friendly but she definitely was a woman that enjoyed having someone by the balls.

As I invited them in, they quickly found the living room and jumped right in to the conversation.

"Gino you got yourself some nice digs here," said Vinnie. "I assume your lady did all the decorating," he said with a smile looking at me. I took it as him showing respect towards me. "No. Gino did it all himself and when he was done he did my place too," said Tommy. We all laughed. "Gino, I can see why you kept her secret. She's beautiful," said Sonny. "Thanks Love," I said. Gino seemed relaxed and composed around the others. Despite still being a tad uncomfortable with the age difference he soaked up the acceptance of his allies. "So how you doing Sonny? Did you enjoy your trip in from Chicago?" Gino asked. "You can only be as comfortable as you make yourself. Anyway Gino, the Old Man said I could pick up some cash from you," he said. Gino shot a look at me and back at Sonny. It was as if he got caught with his hand in the cookie jar. No one knew Gino kept me in the dark. I just sat quietly. "Sure Sonny. Anything you need, just tell me," Gino said. "The usual would be fine," said Sonny. "Sure, no problem Sonny. Joie go in the bedroom and get my brown suede jacket," he said while pouring himself a glass of Bourbon. I had never seen Gino drink Whiskey before. It was nice to see him open up a bit in front of me. I came from the bedroom with the jacket and handed it to him. The others had struck up a conversation while Gino pulled out a few wads of cash. He handed it to Sonny and said, "Here you go. No need to count it. It's all there like usual." Sonny nodded his head. "I know Gino. You're a good man. Now we need to talk about something else. The Old Man needs a drop from the Reserve. Our usual courier can't do it. He got popped last week. We need someone the Feds wouldn't know; someone who's unexpected and new." "Gino maybe we can find a guy from the streets, a hood that's looking for some action," said Sal. "Shouldn't be too hard. Everybody is looking for a piece of something." "I'll do it," I said. The other kept chatting among them as if I hadn't said anything. "I'll do it!" I said loudly. Suddenly the room fell quiet. Gino shot a look at me. "What are you talking about?" Gino said. "I'll do it. I'll do anything for you Gino. Why not? You helped me. I want to help you out," I said. I did have my loyalty to Gino but more so it was about the action. I was tired of sitting in the house all the time. It was like living in a glass case and this doll was ready for some fun. With the conversation around, it didn't take much to clue me in that they were all a part of something big and I wasn't about to sit in the side lines. "Gino, it's brilliant," said Vinnie. "No one knows her. She could be in and out and handle the business in no time," he said. "I don't like the idea," said Gino. "I don't want Joie out there." "Well if the girl wants in and wants to put her neck on the line then accept that she's a big girl," said Gracie. She had some moxie but Gino looked at her like she was about to be a dead dog on the street. She was quick to keep her mouth shut after that. "Joie, you think you can handle it?" asked Sonny. "If I can handle a polish from my Father, there's nothing that I can't take," I said. "Okay Joie, you win. I'll have you do the drop tomorrow," Gino said. "Then it's settled. Joie does the drop and all is right in the world again." The rest of the night went by without any more business talk. We ate and drank and enjoyed the night. I had no clue what to expect in the morning but I was up for anything.

"If you're going to do this, I want you to look the part," Gino said. He had me put on a black pants suit. He wanted me to appear like a business woman. I pulled my hair up and put on my best pair of pearls. My makeup was flawless. I didn't really know what I was about to do but that didn't mean I couldn't look damn good doing it. When I was done getting ready, Gino did a once over on me. "You look like a banker. You look great," he said. "You sure you want to do this?" "Gino, I'll be fine," I said reassuringly. "A silver limousine is going to pick you up outside. Follow the instructions of the driver. Do everything he says to do. I've known him a very long time. He won't cross you. Here's an envelope. After the pick-up, the driver is going to take you to a bank. Go inside and ask for the manager.

Hand her the envelope and she'll know what to do. Joie, you better be smart about this and be safe. I'll meet up with you afterwards." His instructions seemed simple enough and I was pretty quick on the uptake. "I got it," I said. I was eager to do this for Gino. I had been with him for almost a year and it was the first time he had asked me to run an errand. In a way I felt I owed this to him. He looked out of our windows and saw the limo pull up. "The car is here." I grabbed my jacket and gave him a kiss. "Don't worry baby. I won't let you down," I said and headed towards the door. I could feel Gino's eyes on me as I left. He watched from the window as the driver opened the door and I got inside.

A few blocks before the Federal Reserve the driver said, "Lay down on the floor. Trust me you don't want to be spotted." I did as I was instructed to do and got low. He let me know to stay there until we were inside a garage. "Okay, you can get up now. There's a man at the end of garage waiting on you. Take the bags he gives you and hand him this," he said. The driver handed me an envelope that felt like it had cash inside. "If he asks who sent you tell him the Old Man did." I sat up, adjusted my clothing and reached for the handle of the car door. I could feel sensations going through my body as I was walking. The thing I found most odd, however, was I wasn't afraid. The abuse I went through by the hands of my

Father knocked any kind of fear out of me. If I could take a polishing from him and still stand, there wasn't anything in this world to be frightened of. I tucked the envelope under my arm. Walking up the aisle in the parking garage, I spotted a man in a dark brown suit standing calmly. He took a cigarette out of his breast pocket and lit it. As I approached, I felt his eyes scanning my body. He was probably looking for a gun. He nodded at me and impulsively I nodded back. Before he could ask, I just started speaking. "The Old Man sent me," I said. I almost felt power in what I said, like a Boss. I could see the look in his face turn straight to business with hearing those words. "You got my envelope?" he asked. "Of course, he wouldn't have sent me without it," I said as if I had been doing this for years. He placed two bags on the ground in front of me. I could hear a familiar sound come from them as they touched the ground. I handed him the envelope. He opened it and scanned quickly over what was inside then nodded and calmly walked away. I stood for a moment, partly because I was unsure of my next move and partly because I didn't know this man. I didn't want to give him the chance to get the jump on me from behind. As he approached the end of garage I saw him press an elevator button and step inside. Watching the doors close, I instinctively picked up the bags and walked towards the limousine. I felt power inside of myself. Getting in the car the driver said,

"Did you get them?" "Yeah I got them. What's next?" I asked. "Now we go to the bank." Though there was curiosity I knew better than to open the bags. "Lay low till I tell you it's safe." Again, I followed instructions. I figured he must have been doing this long enough so who the hell was I to question him. Once we were well outside of the garage and several streets down he told me I could sit up.

We drove for quite some time and approached a street in Miami that I learned to enjoy shopping on since I had been with Gino. He pulled up in front of the Continental National Bank down off of South West First Street in the heart of Miami. It was Cuban American owned, which could have been one of the main reasons why it was selected. He told me to take the bags inside and ask for the Branch Manager, Evita Castellanos. He said she would know what to do and who sent me. He handed me another envelope and told me he was going to wait for me outside. I took a quick glance over myself to freshen up my makeup, and then with bags in hand I got out of the car. I walked up the stairs in front of the bank and pushed the door open with new confidence. I looked around the Lobby almost instinctively and scanned the layout. Tellers at the windows were assisting the customers, employees were scattered about at desks with people. Out of the corner of my eye, I spotted a security guard. He was old and fat. He looked like he was ready to retire at any moment. Cash was flowing in and out of this place and he was supposedly the guardian of it all. The place was a sitting duck.

"May I help you?" said a man dressed in a tan suit with a royal blue tie. He was an employee of the bank with a very pleasant appearance. "Yes. I'm looking for Evita Castellanos. She's expecting me," the words slipped out of my mouth with such steadiness even I believed myself. It was like I was in a play portraying the main character. It was me but I was someone else. "I'll be more than happy to find Evita for you. Would you like to have a seat in the mean time?" I nodded and he led me to a row of wooden chairs in the back of the branch. After a few minutes I spotted him approaching with a woman. She was olive complexion which was highlighted by the red skirt suit she was wearing. Her dark hair was pulled back in a tight neat bun. She had a look about her that made it obvious to the rest of the world that she was in control. I have always admired women in power. I never found women who were meek to be of any use. What sense did it make to sit back and let people step on you? That damn sure was never going to be me. I remembered Gino's words about looking the part. Now was my chance, I stood up to be eye to eye with her as she greeted me.

"Hello there. I'm Evita," she said with the perfect smile. "Hello Evita, you've been expecting me," I said calmly and handed her the envelope from the driver. She looked back at me with a glance that read "game on." I could tell she was well versed on what was to happen next even though I was clueless. "Right this way," she said. "Of course," I stepped out of her way so she could lead me to the area where the safety deposit boxes were held. She took a set of keys from her pocket and opened up the wall covering which contained a box. She pulled the long container from its resting place and set it on the table in from me. "You will find everything in order. I will make sure your deposit is handled right away. Will there be anything else I can assist you with?" she asked me as if I had been doing this for years. I pulled a package out of the container making sure to appear as if I knew what to do with it. "No, that will be all today. Thank you." "As always, it's a pleasure doing business," she said to me. I gave her a dignified nod.

Each step I took towards the exit of the bank was more bold and powerful than the last. I could feel the assertiveness grow inside of me. It felt like I was beginning to transform in to what I was meant to be, in to what I was built for. The feelings of strength and power were better than any high I could have. I got in to the limousine and the driver quickly turned around to see my face. "Did you get it?" he asked. "Of course I did," I handed him the package from the safety deposit box. I never did learn the contents of it but it really wasn't important. I completed the mission that was given to me. "Well done," he said. "One last stop to make. This time you stay in the car," he gave his orders very clearly. "Where are we heading to now?" I asked out of sheer curiosity. "The airport."

Pulling up to Miami's International Airport, I watched out of my window as the planes were taking off. I wondered for a brief moment where some of those people were headed and what new adventures they were about to have. It was almost symbolic to me. The driver parked the car and instructed me to stay put. I took advantage of the bottles of champagne in the back of the car while I waited. It was a small celebration to me and the day's successful events. The element of danger was never something that entered in to my thought pattern. It was completely overlooked. It was all just a job to me like dropping off the dry cleaning. Soon the driver returned and we were on our way to Gino. I had hopes that the brief time I spent out was enough for me to prove to Gino I wasn't as fragile as he thought I was. Hell, my Father taught me how to be hard. I guess I should thank him for that.

Pulling up outside of my apartment building, we found Gino there smoking a cigarette and awaiting my arrival. "Right on time," he said as we walked up. "How did she do?" he asked the driver. "No snags and it's all done," he responded. Gino reached in his pocket, pulled out a wad of cash and handed it to him. The driver took the money and went on his way. "Good job Joie, here this is for you," he handed me some money too. I knew better then to count it. Gino was always generous to me. "It was nothing. Now let's go get some food going for dinner," I said as I headed toward the steps of our building. Gino just looked in my direction. He had seen in that moment that I had some moxie. I let the day's events roll off me like water off a duck's back. Gino took my hand before I could go up the stairs. "Joie, you did a good job today. It's nice to know I can count on you," he said as he looked straight in to my eyes. "Anytime Gino," I replied. "I may use you again. The jobs would be just like today. In and out, easy work. I'll pay you but business is business, our home life is separate. You understand?" "Gino, I understand clearly. I'll be fine. No worries. Now let's get upstairs," I said with a smile. I was ready to change clothes and go pick up Nikki with Gino. I may have loved the power I felt for the day, but my instant kryptonite was being a Mother.

Joie Miami

## Chapter Seven:  Tailor Made

Somewhere inside of me, I knew Gino was good for me.  I knew I was going to be financially set for life, I knew my child was never going to have to struggle for anything, and I knew who I was as a person was about to fully evolve.  Others may have looked at my life and what I was beginning to involve myself with as ludicrous or even too dangerous.  Truthfully, I couldn't have given two shits when it came to other people's opinions of me or my life choice for that matter.  None of them had experienced a childhood like mine.  None of them faced the abuse I went through.  I wasn't about to go back to having nothing.  I was ready to sit and eat nails if I had to just to make sure I would survive.  To prove even further to Gino that I was ready, I took on his last name.  I became Joie Talarico.

For a while my errands for Gino were just like that first run.  A limo would arrive and off I went.  I handled the pick-ups and drops from the Federal Reserve to the Continental National Bank.  It became very standard routine for me.  At the end of every run, I was then off to pick up Nikki, do a little shopping and get dinner ready. It was like having a normal nine to five and as with every job comes expansion and growth.

Gino began looking for new places to have the drops made. He didn't want to stay with just one place in case the heat came. He was looking for a new connection. I suggested my own bank. I had been doing business there for a while. I knew the ins and outs of it. I knew the employees and managers. I knew I could convince someone from the inside to work with the outside. Gino was a little reluctant with the idea but I was soon able to pitch him on it. One thing I knew I was good at was being charismatic. I knew if there was a crowd, I could work it. That's why I was so good at being a waitress. I could charm my way in to a nice fat tip. If I could get Gino on board with my plan then I knew I could make it work. One thing we both agreed on quickly was a dry run needed to be done. A test to ensure my idea was solid.

The testing phase of the plan wasn't that far off, for a week we went over what the strategy would be. Gino came up with an idea of giving me some cash and a few checks; some were made out to me, the rest were made out to unknown people by unknown companies. I was to find a bank employee to befriend, convince him or her to cash the checks and keep his or her mouth shut. A small percentage of the profits would be given for the quality of silence. Once we had a small foot in the door, the next step would be to buy out a Manager. As usual a driver would pick me up and drop me off. He would also be my back up in case things got a little hot under the collar. I was done planning it all out with Gino; the time had come to set it all in motion.

As I got dressed for my mission, Gino was out visiting with the Old Man and getting the documents and cash needed for the job. I hadn't met the Old Man just yet, but from the conversations of others I imagined what he might have looked like. One thing I did know, he was about business and making money just like Gino. The Old Man must have liked our idea because it wasn't long before Gino came back with all that was needed and I was on my way.

Inside the vehicle provided, which was a beautiful silver Jaguar, I noticed the windows to the car were dark. No one could see what was going on inside but I could look out on the world. It was the perfect vehicle for me. As the car came to a slow stop, I seen we were in front of my bank. The driver came to my door and opened it. I stepped out and put some sunglasses on. I didn't want anyone to be able to read my face. "I'll be right outside if you need me." "Thank you," I replied but I knew it really wasn't necessary. I was pretty confident this was going to be simple.

I walked inside and found my mark right off the bat. A female teller that has known me for a while was my easiest prey. Not only did she know me but she heard of who I was with and assumed who backed me up. She truthfully was afraid of me and every inch of her body told me was having an anxiety attack just from looking at me. I made small chit chat to try and ease her nerves.

"Hi sweetie, how are you today? I have a few checks I need cashed," I handed the documents through the small opening at the bottom of the window. She looked over them and her eyes shot at me quickly. The fact that I didn't move an inch and kept my demeanor the same made her even more uneasy. "Absolutely ma'am," she said quietly and kept her composure as best as she could. While she was handling the transaction, I was scanning over her and looking for signs that she would give a tip off. I found her name tag, it read; *It's my pleasure to assist you, Heather.* How fitting and ironic, I thought and couldn't stop the smirk that formed on my face. "Ma'am, I believe it's all here. Would you like to count it?" "No, that's okay Heather. I trust you," I said and gave her a glance that I knew she could feel down to her spine. "Yes Ma'am. Would there be anything else for today?" she asked. "Not now, but I will be seeing you again soon. Thank you for your assistance," I said and gave her a cocky smile. I left the bank and headed towards the car. Another successfully completed mission for me. It was also another step closer to obtaining what I wanted most for myself- power. My vision of myself didn't include the role of housewife or mistress. I wanted more. Eventually, I grew enough confidence to walk in to a AmeriFirst Bank branch located off of Biscayne Boulevard in North Miami and recruited the Vice President.

Having the bank contacts meant I could bring in more money and watch the dollars grow. Soon I had routines I set it up to where I would visit the banks often and make deposits. I took money from accounts that were established for Diverlandia and Juliania.

On paper both corporations, Diverlandia and Juliania were owned by a man named Carlos Toll. He was a real man in Panama. He has a clean record and he was very poor. It made him an easy target for the Mafia. The Mob would find those who were dead broke and send in someone with a trusting face to convince them to they would provide a better lifestyle for them. Carlos Toll was paid off for the use of his name in which he bought some real estate and cars for his family. In return, he established a few more fake corporations. Money may not buy happiness but it can make life a hell of lot easier and Carlos Toll knew it.

I set up a safety deposit box there to store jewelry and guns. Withdrawals I made were always under ten thousand dollars at a time so that the IRS wouldn't be attracted and taxes would not be paid. Each transaction was handled smoothly. We worked it out to where I would walk in and catch my contact's eye. I would simply raise a finger and they knew what to do. My relationships were solid for two reasons. The first was each contact was paid one to two hundred dollars a transaction. The second reason was because I made sure to instill the knowledge that if a word was spoken to authorities they would no longer exist to tell stories. I was now a money courier for the Mafia but I wasn't about to stop there. I had an in and I planned to hold on to it because in spite of all I was doing, Gino was getting the credit. I wanted to become a valuable asset in the eyes of the Mafia leaders. I wanted a place at the table in an all man's world.

I watched Gino like a hawk. I observed the things he did and why. I made mental notes of his processes. In the beginning, he would disappear when he did his business, but eventually he brought me with him to see how he moved. I became aware of everything he did. I was anxious to learn it all. I learned how to launder money, cash checks from dummy corporations based in the Cayman Islands, buy apartments, houses and cars under assumed names, load planes to smuggle cash, pharmaceuticals, obtained by having a doctor and pharmacist on payroll, and guns between the United States and Panama. I would chauffer mobsters, cater their funerals and weddings. Nothing I learned and did, no matter how illegal, phased me. It was all no big deal. I had never considered the dangers involved. It was like I was a working stiff. I would handle the work that was thrown my way and still make it home in time for supper. Things were going smoothly and I was gaining more trust from Gene and the others involved. I became known for my loyalty which is highly important when working with the Mafia. Some days I would wake up, have my morning coffee and by the end of the day thousands of dollars and diamonds bigger than anyone had ever seen had traveled through my fingertips.

Gino was delighted in the growth and potential that I demonstrated. He began to open up more to me. On several occasions, Gino and I had conversations about business. One thing he clued me in on was the fact that he kept a secret ledger. Gino didn't keep this ledger for "insurance" just in case the other Mafia members became unhappy with him or turned against him. He kept the ledger to keep track of things for himself. The contents of the ledger included information on meetings, secret transactions and clandestine activities that went on in the "Organization." He divulged that several entries included money that had been hidden in the

Cayman Islands, which was made by the proud investments of the Mafia and my hard work with the laundered money. Gino warned me if the book fell in to the wrong hands the ramifications would be far reaching and very devastating.

It was also because of his ledger I learned that Gino never skimmed much Mob money, but he did run his own side games to make profits for himself. Gino and I thought a lot alike when it came to branching out. His ring was of small time thieves and drug dealers he recruited from the streets or from jobs they had previously performed for him. Soon, he had me picking up money from them and dropping off the next supply of pharmaceuticals or guns. The profits were a few thousand dollars a week made up from the drug sales and robberies. It sounds like a lot but for the Mafia it was peanuts. Pick-ups and drop offs were casually in the open outdoors. Our favorite pick up locations were various car washes in town. I would literally drive one of our vehicles, which we had many of, through the wash and make the exchanges. With the Mafia everything was about appearance and we stayed riding clean. Lincolns, Cadillacs, Jaguars, and BMWs all sparkling like they were right off of the show room floor.

Gino instilled enough knowledge in me to where I could run things when he needed to go out of town or was ill. Gene began to get sick often.

He had moments where it was difficult for him to even get out of bed. It was those times where I would have his back. He had me set up with my own team made up of guys he hand-selected for specific reasons. Most importantly, he knew he could trust them if something went down. He made sure they weren't pussies. They were guys who would take out their own Mothers if they had to. Gino had more smarts than most of his fellow soldiers and I was taking advantage of it. Soon, I was one of very few mob women who knew everything that went down. I wasn't going to be like the other mafia women playing on their man's dollar. I was never going to be satisfied by being under another person's control. Gene may have thought he was grooming me to become an asset for him and Larner, but I had other plans.

# Joie Miami

## Chapter Eight:  Home Sweet Home

Arriving back from a "business" trip in Chile in 1974, Gino came home and couldn't wait to see me and Nikki.  He scooped her up and gave her a hug.  To him, she had become the apple of his eye.  "Hey babe," he said and laid a big kiss on me.  "Hey you!" I chuckled.  He seemed so excited and full of energy.  "So I take it everything went well on your trip?" I asked.  "Better than well.  I've got a surprise for you and Nikki."  "What is it?" I asked. "It's pretty big one.  You might want to sit down for this," he teased.  "I'm good.  Just tell me." I said with total curiosity dripping from my pores.  "Why don't I just show you?" he said.  He pulled some papers with pictures on them from his coat pocket.  Looking closely, I realized it was pictures of a house I had been eyeing for a while, a four bedroom modern ranch style home with a unique crescent shaped layout.  "What is this Gino?" I said looking over the home.  "Well, I would call it our home," he said and took the keys out of his shirt pocket to wave in front of me.  "Oh my god! Oh Gino! This is amazing.  When do we move in it?"  "As soon as you want babe!" he said. I couldn't believe my wildest fantasies were coming true. Nothing seemed to stand in our way. We truly were unstoppable together.

I loved our new place. It was the highlight of the neighborhood we lived in. For the first few weeks we were there, I spent my time painting the house, cleaning and situating the furniture just how I wanted it, and enjoying all the new housewarming presents that were sent by Gino's associates. It really did feel like it was home. Soon Gino's boys were stopping by for coffee and homemade pastries. They would even stop by just to check up on me and Nikki when Gino was out of town. I was so happy in our new house. I still couldn't believe that Gino had surprised me with such a beautiful place and best of all- both of our names were on the paperwork. The landscape was breathtaking and in such a nice neighborhood. It was really a great place for Nikki to grow up. Things began to feel like a normal life until a man by the name of Jimmy Russell, a foot soldier for "The Old Man," showed up at my door. Gino wasn't home and Nikki was at a sleep over.

Jimmy was standing in my door way with a mink rug rolled up. "How you doing Joie?" he said when I opened the door. "I'm good

Jimmy," I said. I was a little puzzled by his appearance and curious about the rug. "Can I come in?" he asked. "Sure," I said and stepped out of his way. He carried the rug in to the living room. "Gino isn't home," I said to him. "That's okay I can wait on him. I need to talk to you too. I have to ask for a favor from you," he said. I had known Jimmy through passing from my operations for Gino. He had never really asked me for anything before. "I'm listening," I replied. That's when he told me about a situation that occurred in Panama. He said there were some problems and complications arose that forced him to shoot a police officer. He also clued me in to the fact that a big pay off went down to get him back in to the United States courtesy of The Old Man. Jimmy reached in to his coat and pulled out an envelope with twenty thousand dollars inside and asked me to do him the favor of opening up a bank account under an assumed name so no one would know about it and he would have the money whenever he needed it. He asked me to keep it between us. He didn't want Gino or anyone else knowing about it. I gave him my word and went to put the money away for safe keeping until I could get out to one of the banks.

It wasn't long before Gino came home and saw Jimmy sitting on the couch awaiting his arrival. He also noticed the mink rug rolled up and sitting on the floor. "Gino, Jimmy came to see you," I said. "I see," he looked over at Jimmy with a cold stare. "By the way Jimmy, is that a real mink rug?" I asked. After all, I was female and had a passion for the finer things thanks to Gene. "Yeah it is. You can have it if you want. Consider it a housewarming gift from me to you." "Thanks. Well, I'll leave you two alone to discuss things," I knew better than to stick around when Gene had that look on his face. Jimmy stayed for all of about 20 minutes. After he left, I went back in to the living room to check on Gino. He had unrolled the rug and inside was a machine gun with United States military markings on it. It was like something out of a movie. I kept quiet but my eyes were on it. Gino shook my concentration when he said, "here's your rug. Where do you want me to put it?" For a while that rug from Jimmy stayed under our dining room table. Later on when I needed money, I sold it for two thousand dollars. I kept my word to James Russell and took the envelope to the bank. I even opened up the account for him. Sad to say, I never saw him again after that night. I assumed that he was put out to pasture. From time to time I would wonder about his wife and children back in Panama. I even wanted to find a way to send the money he left to them but I didn't dare try. I knew better. Gino was loving and very giving to those he cared about. The flip side to his personality was cold and calculated. He was able to give the order to have someone taken out without blinking than come home and play with Nikki. I knew if he had to Gino would have given the order to kill Russell's wife and kids without any problem. That side of Gino was one I didn't want to be close to but I knew it was lurking. The heartless side of him was something no one should have seen. Like a shark, it would surface and cause more fear and destruction than anyone could imagine.


*Gino's callus side was demonstrated very clearly to me with the execution style murders of Vincenzo Ruotolo Jr.'s parents- Lee and Vincenzo Ruotolo Sr. Vinnie Jr. used to work for Gene on the Angelina Laura and the Costa Lines ships that the mafia used to export and import on. Vinnie Jr.'s main job was to keep an eye on all of the business transactions that occurred. Vinnie's problem was that he wanted to have a side line game of his own but he was tampering with Gino's turf. Once Gene discovered that Vinnie Jr. was dealing drugs on the ships on his own, he had him removed. The Old Man caught wind of Vinnie's actions and despite what he had done, Hyman wanted him to stay on board to work off a debt that his parents owed. Whether the money owed was borrowed or money that was to be laundered was never mentioned around me. Gino placed Vinnie Jr. back on the boats under Larner's command but Vinnie held a grudge. His feelings towards The Old Man and Gene were never kept hidden and eventually it got him kicked completely to the curb with a warning*

*to keep a good distance. Knowing the debt was still owed by his parents*

*and wanting to show off a little bit that he had skills of his own to make it,*

*Vinnie Jr. and five others, four men and a woman, from the boats*

*collaborated together and hit a hotel in Miami Beach called "The Seasons".*

*They stole half a million in money and jewelry. The loot was to be divided*

*amongst all that were involved. Instead, Vinnie Jr. took off with everything.*

*Everyone knew Vinnie Jr. to be a loose cannon and no one was surprised by*

*his actions. Weeks later one of the crew, the woman, involved in the*

*robbery turned state's evidence and ratted everyone out.*

*Soon the phone calls began to our home. The calls were sporadic*

*from Vinnie Jr. begging us for help. He said he was lying in the swamps and*

*needed his fingertips burned off so no one could identify his prints. He was*

*like a trapped animal. I told Gino we should help him since the half of a*

*million that was stolen had not been accounted for. There could have been*

*a piece in it for us. We knew if he turned himself in the chance of our cut*

*would be void. Gino actually agreed with me but he didn't want to make a*

*move without Hyman Larner's green light. "Vinnie's calling for help. He's*

*laying low in the swamps and needs some back up," Gino said. Larner's*

*position was very clear. He didn't want Gino to get involved. He said Vinnie was too hot and to stay away. Gino called Vinnie back and made it known*

*he was unable to assist him. That's when Vinnie started pressuring me to*

*help him out without Gene. "Fuck it, the least I could do is bring you a gun,"*

*I told him.*

*I left the next morning, after Gene was gone. Taking I-95 South, I*

*watched through the windshield as the clouds began to gather together.*

*Gorgeous pinks and peaches were radiating like a Caribbean Carnival*

*Cruise advertisement. After about an hour on the interstate, I took the*

*Tamiani Trail for twenty minutes, bringing me to the Everglades. I came to*

*an abandoned souvenir shop and circled around behind it. Branches clawed*

*at the sides of my car, the dense canopy putting me in a dusty twilight,*

*continuing for a few minutes, until the narrow dirt road dead-ended at a*

*thicket of mahogany and fiddlewood. In the rearview mirror, I touched up my*

*makeup then waited for Vinnie to emerge. Coming out of the thicket, gaunt*

*and frightened Vinnie Jr. was shaking and looked like a homeless bum.*

*Knowing the risk, I got out of my car. I walked up to Vinnie and hugged him.*

*I was happy to see him, even if he looked like shit. I handed him a 38 nickel-*

*plated, unregistered firearm. In the back of my head, I was still thinking of*

*scoring some of the robbery loot. "Thank you JoAnn. I owe you one," he*

*said. I would have appreciated a couple grand for coming out to his side but*

131

Vinnie's mind was still on escaping. "Come with me JoAnn." "Are you crazy Vinnie? I can't do that. I got a good thing going." I knew better than to destroy what I had for someone that was on the run. I also knew that if Gino found out he would kill us both. "I'm scared Joie. What should I do?" "You have a lot of money right now Vinnie. Take it and find a someone to do plastic surgery. Leave the country." I had hoped Vinnie would talk about the cash but he never took the bait. Instead he took the gun I brought him and decided to head to Atlanta. He hid in a friend's trailer. From the story that was later told to me, a police woman showed up at the trailer to ask his friend about a traffic violation. Vinnie thought she was there to arrest him. He pulled the office inside at gunpoint and told her to shut up. "Listen, I'm not gonna hurt you," he said "I just want to get away." The police woman had no clue who he was and Vinnie soon realized he made a horrible mistake. He knocked her completely out and took off. He found a phone booth and called me hysterical. This time I made it crystal clear to him I wasn't coming to help him and to turn himself in. "Okay JoAnn. I can't do this anymore. I give up. All I want is to see my parents first. If I'm going to go down, at least I can show them I'm alright. My father is sick. He has a weak heart. I know this must be killing him," he said. The line went dead after that. Apparently, he called his parents and told them he wanted to see them before he went to prison. He asked them to set the deal up with the police department. A few hours later, local authorities in Atlanta picked up Vinnie Jr. and brought him by helicopter to Miami. They had a trooper vehicle escort him to his parent's house.

Vinnie was sentenced to ten years in prison for robbery, assault and kidnapping of the police woman. He wound up doing five years with time off for good behavior. The guards were probably paid off by his parents before they died. Unfortunately for Vinnie Jr. one of the guys from the robbery ended up in the same cell block as him. On a daily basis he would question Vinnie about the money. Then the threats started. "If you don't give us the money we'll kill your dog." "I'm not giving you shit!" The guy reached a contact on the outside and a few days later Vinnie's parents informed him that their beloved German Sheppard was stabbed and gutted like a fish. Vinnie still wouldn't give up the location of the money. "Give up the money or we'll kill your parents next." Vinnie responded by saying "Fuck you!"

Gene came home one night and told me he needed me for a special job. "What is it babe?" I asked with total curiosity. He instructed me to begin funeral arrangements for a husband and wife. He said he wanted it to look respectful and filled with flowers. "Oh my god! Who died?" I asked.

He didn't respond to me right away. Gene took the phone and told me to call Lee and Vinnie Sr.'s family. Being with the mafia, we had just as many connections as the FBI and could find a needle in a haystack much better. "No problem babe." I called around and was able to reach a few members of the Ruotolo family. Gene informed them in Italian that Lee and Vinnie Sr. had been killed execution style. Execution style killings differ from regular killings because it's just about the murder. The victim could be wearing a fifty thousand dollar Rolex, holding a bag of loot, a two thousand dollar briefcase and decked out in expensive jewels, but the killer leaves it all behind to send a message that all they wanted was the person dead.

Lee and Vinnie Sr. ran a mom and pop restaurant down off of Biscayne Boulevard. It was the same restaurant that Gino and I frequented. They had just closed up shop for the night and were heading home. They got out of their car and were walking up the stairs to their apartment. Before they could make it inside they were shot in their heads. Their faces were shattered. Lee died with her key in the door and her husband right behind her. The killer shot each of them in the chest to ensure they were dead. Everyone assumed they were killed by the people with whom Vinnie Jr. owed money from the robbery. At least that's what Gene and the other mafia boys wanted the police to think. It makes a great back story, the killing *was revenge. The truth was a lot less complicated. Vinnie Jr.'s parents still owed Hyman Larner. When Gino went to collect on the debt they always responded the same way- they were broke. Everyone suspected they were lying. Gino found out Vinnie's parents sent the money to family members in Italy.*

*Making the funeral arrangements was hard for me to do. I loved Lee and Vinnie Sr. I loved walking in the door of the restaurant and head straight for the kitchen. Vinnie Sr. was always cooking something delicious. "Pop, how are you?" I'd ask. "How's your heart?" I knew he struggled with his heart problems. "What you wanna eat, Joie," he's ask in his broken English, with a smile. "I'm gonna fix you a nice dinna," he would say. He'd make me something extra special and always off the menu. He'd always fix something nice up for Nikki too; usually it was her favorite dish veal piard. He was so sweet and loving. After he was killed, I thought of how he'd just undergone a successful triple bypass surgery. His wife, Lee would always be in front of the register with a cigarette dangling from her lips. She acted tough, but the truth was she was a sweet lady. It made me so sad to know they were gone. To Gino, it just meant we needed to find a new place to eat. Business was just that to Gino; no feelings, no regrets, no emotions were granted the opportunity to surface unless he decided it was time.*

135

Gino had his ways of dealing with his dark side. I think that's part of the reason why he also chose to take me and Nikki in. We were his light at the end of the dark tunnel. We were the silver lining in the gray clouds. Though Gino had a son of his own, Nikki was his happiness. She loved him and they had a true father and daughter relationship. Our house contained a real family.

Joie Miami

Chapter Nine:  The Old Man and Mert

Hyman Larner, known as The Old Man, was truly the Jew of all

Jews.  He had to have been since he dealt with people like Sam Giancana,

the Chicago Mob boss.  Larner was highly intelligent and knew how to keep

a low profile.  He was known as a concigliere or an advisor.  I preferred to

think of him as a negotiator. Hyman was the liaison between Noriega and

the Mafia.  His relationship with Noriega grew from a very smart deal to

expand operations to Latin America.  Soon the smuggling and gambling

headquarters were based out of Panama in a home set high in the hills,

made entirely of glass and surrounded by flowers.  It was nicknamed "The

Glasshouse" and was owned personally by Larner.  By 1966, those

operations expanded even further into Saudi Arabia.

Hyman Larner and his wife, Mert, decided to make Miami, Florida

their home.  They bought an apartment in a very exclusive condo

development, hired an expensive decorator and purchased the best of

everything.  It was from this condo, Hyman helped to make the Mafia

millions of dollars, while Mert played with her thousand dollars worth of china sets. The Old Man did everything for her. He made sure she didn't have to do much of anything. Mert was never very good at being domestic. She had people that cleaned for her. When it came to meals for her and Hyman she had someone to cook for them too. Ralph "Chop" Di Costanza was there as a personal chef and from what I heard and had the pleasure to experience; he did a damn good job.

*Gino once told me that Larner had a plane come in from Panama. He and Chop loaded it with coins for the casinos in Latin America and pharmaceuticals. They also brought on board lobsters and other prime seafood from Joe's Stone Crab Shack. They flew the plane back to Panama and Chop cooked dinner for the Mob and Noriega.*

Hyman and Mert had the finer things in life but the one thing money couldn't buy them was a healthy son. Their son, Mort, was dying of cancer. By the time Gino brought me to meet Hyman and Mert, Mort was coming very close to the end of his battles. When Gino introduced me to Mert we sat and spoke for hours, not as women of the Mafia, but as Mothers. She confided in me that she was worried about her son and tending to him was all she could focus on. She was worried about her home as well. During the times she was away, she wanted to make sure her plants were taken care of well and things were running smoothly. That's where I came in. Mert could have paid anyone to look after things for her but she had a huge distrust of people. She didn't like hiring outside help. She had severe arthritis, was losing her only biological child, and was stone cold hearted to everyone, but I somehow won her over. After our meeting, she felt she could trust me. Truthfully, she may have had money and power but I felt sorry for her and respected her. My sympathies were stemmed from the mother within me. I couldn't imagine what is was like for her to get up every day not knowing if it was going to be the last time she saw her son. Money may buy many things but it can't stop the last breath from escaping a loved one's body. Nikki had always been my joy, my heart and a small piece of my soul on Earth. They say when a child is born, a mother is as well. Mert may have had the most expensive and finest of everything money could buy, but I knew deep within her she would have traded it all in for a healthy child. In a way, I didn't mind helping her out. I knew if I took care of her, she would take care of me. There was something else I would also benefit from; having an in. While the rich are busy being rich, the servants are always busy learning all of their secrets. I knew if I kept quiet and did what was asked of me I could also keep my ear in tune to what was going on directly from the source. Information was the best thing for me to walk away with.

After our initial meeting, Mert had me running errands for her right away. What I did for her was very different from my work that I did with Gene. It was easy stuff. Most of the work was cleaning houses and apartments, running dry cleaning, watering plants, bringing in the mail, and picking up and dropping off items like jewelry. One time, she asked me to pick up a completely see through bag of her jewels. There truly were some gorgeous pieces that looked like they belonged in glass casing. I could have taken something and she probably would not have missed it. But I never would have stolen from my own kind. I had no need to. Gino provided everything I wanted. That was one of the reasons why I was so trust worthy.

It was while I ran errands for Mert that I learned about Hyman Larner's relationship with Manuel Noriega. I may not have known exactly what they did out in Panama, but I did know what they did in Miami. I knew where Noriega and his family would be staying when they came to town and who would accompany them. I'd find an apartment or house, if they didn't have one already and make sure it was cleaned to perfection. I knew what food was to be stocked and served. Fresh fruit and flowers were never in short supply, the mini bars were always full and anything else they wanted was picked up. Hell, I even knew what fabric softener they liked using for laundry. If they needed a pick-up at the airport or customs, to go shopping, or just for night out at a restaurant I set up the transportation. This was information that no one else was privy to.

Nikki was getting older now. She was growing in to a beautiful young girl and had an interest in the Spanish language. When Noriega came to town I would sometimes bring her with me and have her quietly fill me in on things that were said that I didn't understand. Nikki was always a smart kid. I admired her for that and she never let anyone know she was Mommy's little spy. The information Nikki passed on to me was helpful in staying a step ahead. Like the saying goes, "by any means necessary."

My hard work for Mert didn't go unnoticed. Hyman felt comfortable with me too. Soon he had me running errands as well. His errands were a bit a little more in depth. He had me transporting pharmaceuticals. Thousands of valiums, Percocets, barbiturates, narcotics would be in and out of my car. He would give me lists and I'd go to one of two local pharmacies in Miami Beach. I would simply bring the list that was provided up to the counter, someone from behind the counter would fill in a prescription form and then hand me the drugs. Once the drugs were in my possession, I would either have to deliver them for a fee to people in the

141

Miami area or arrange for shipment to the Old Man's address in Panama. Shipping the drugs out of the country was always interesting to me. Gino had worked out a smart process. He built small wooden boxes referred to as "coffins." Sometimes, I would help with building them when the shipments were large. The coffins would be loaded up with coins, money, alcohol, lobster and caviar on ice, the drugs from the pharmacies and pure cocaine. Once the coffins were ready we would call our people to meet at the Executive Airport on 36th Street in North Miami, where someone was paid off to look the other way. I'd climb into a truck loaded down with the coffins. I was far from dumb so I always packed heat on me. I wasn't about to sit next to a drunken runner and not be armed. The runner and I would drive the coffins over to a Cessna plane with the hangar code, HP800, inscribed on the side of a wing tip. Gino would be waiting with our team to pack up the plane. Hyman's cousin, Harold Lee would bring in the money made from the pharmaceuticals dealt throughout Panama, Chile and all of South America. The money was used for payroll and payoffs. Money was coming and going from every angle. For months, I enjoyed watching the flow of the dollars pour in like waves in the ocean.

Besides the drug profits, I learned about the earnings from the casinos on cruise ships. Docked off the southern Florida coast were: The

Angelina Laura, The Boheme, the Costa Line ships and the Flavia. Each individual ship not only contained casinos but other money makers like game and vending machines. It was incredible how much was being made so easily. It almost made me laugh once knowing how hard I used to work for petty tips at a restaurant and now I had money traveling through my hands in wads. Every machine on board these ships were serviced by one man only, mine. Gino was a mechanic genius. He even earned the nickname "The Whiz" on board these ships. The Old Man didn't trust anybody else to service his machines. Gino was his right-hand man. The profits from the casinos were supposedly split between Hyman and the Chicago Mob.

One night while at home with Gino the telephone rang. The news provided to us on the other end of that phone was so unexpected and it left me with one of my hardest missions; planning the funeral arrangements for The Old Man and Mert's son. Mort lost his battle to cancer. It was something we all knew would eventually happen but never really thought about or wanted to bring up around his parents. The sound of Mert's tears over her son's passing was hard to swallow. A child is never supposed to pass away before his or her parent. The pain experienced by the loss is simply unbearable. She truly was in no condition to plan the arrangements. The Old Man asked for me to personally see to it. He had heard of the funeral I put together for Lee and Vinnie Sr. and knew I would do a classy job.

At Mort's wake, the heads of the Mafia branches were present. People came from everywhere out of respect for Hyman. The capacity of dominance was overflowing but everyone knew better than to try and show out at that moment. No one dared to even breathe wrong or they knew they would join Mort to the grave. Hyman was like *"il don di professori"* and no one was going to disrespect him at that moment. All the Mafia heads of family were lined in the back of the room. The women and guests were to be seated. Gino had some guys take care of the ushering. As people were seated, I walked in and out over seeing things. I could feel the stares from people. Those that knew me were looking for information. Those that didn't were probably looking me over. Italian funerals were very strict with dress code. I didn't give a shit. I looked respectable in a plain black dress and heels with gold jewelry. Through the sea of people that were present, I could still feel someone was watching me. I caught a glimpse out of the corner of my eye of a man staring right at me. It was Santo Trafficante, the real Godfather of the Mafia, and he was interested in getting to know me.

Joie Miami

## Chapter Ten:  Santo

Santo Trafficante Jr., The Don of all Dons and what I like to consider the last of real big time Mafioso, inherited his power and business connections when his Father, Santo Trafficante Sr., passed away in 1954 of stomach cancer.  Santo Sr. gained power in Florida in the 1930s by having his hands dipped heavily in the bolita lotteries.  Bolita lotteries originated in Cuba and eventually were brought over to Florida by immigrants. The lotteries were supposed to be games of chance.  Balls with numbers on them were poured into bags and bets were placed on which numbers would be drawn out.  Chance usually got affected when someone would pour extra numbers into the bags and rig the games.

Santo Trafficante Sr. became known as the "King of the Bolitas" and his power didn't stop there.  With ties to Charles "Lucky" Luciano, Thomas Lucchese and Meyer Lansky, Santo Sr.'s reach began to spread up the East Coast to New York.  At the height of his father's reign, Santo Trafficante Jr. began showing an interest in the family business.  He studied the ins and outs of organized crime and kept close watch on everything.

*Santo Jr. was classy. He wasn't the regular mobster type. He was someone other mob associates wished they could be. He was low key and grounded with a love for his family no one could light a flame to. He was someone to admire and fear at the same time. He truly was the total package.*

There he was, amongst the sea of other mafia heads, Santo Trafficante Jr. was standing in his refined nature with his eyes upon me. His presence was felt through the energy in the room. It may have been a wake for Mort but Santo was stealing the show. He was someone everybody wanted to speak with and bent over backwards to get his attention. Gino was in line with the rest of the guys waiting for a chance to talk to him. Gino never had to tell me who he was. I was able to put two and two together from the whispers and stares. I was intrigued by him and wanted to get a little closer. His eyes were pulling me in. They told me that there was something he wanted to say to me and I was more than ready to listen. My attraction to men with power has always been strong.

Gene did what he could to make eye contact with Santo. Realizing we were together, Santo granted an invitation to have Gene come sit down and chat for a bit with me at his side. Truthfully, I believe it was his way of getting closer to me so he could check me out. By this point, my name was becoming known around those with connections and power. I was no longer considered just another pretty face or mafia house wife. I was earning my place at the table with the big boys and enjoying the spoils of my riches and hard work. Perhaps it was my tenacity that caused Santo to be just as intrigued with me and I was with him. Perhaps it may have been stories he was hearing from the guys on the streets about a woman sticking her neck out on the line. Maybe it was the idea of a woman gone rogue from the Mafia's view of what a woman should be. Whatever it was that brought us together, I had his attention and he had mine.

Santo, sitting on a Victorian style couch in a small room at the funeral home, had his wife Josephine join us. Josephine Trafficante, also known as Josie, was such a sweet woman with Southern etiquette and the drawl to match. She was heavy set but still a beautiful woman. Though I was now known as someone who was well connected and performed the duties required as a Mafia soldier, I demonstrated I was still a lady by sitting and chatting with Josie. Santo and Gino talked a bit about general business while Josie and I started to get to know each other. As Josie and I were making friendly conversation, Santo jumped in by asking Gino if I was his wife. A slight awkward silence fell over all of us which I broke by simply saying, "I'm Joie, nice to meet you." Santo's eyes were locked on me. Gino noticed it too. Josie wasn't disturbed in any way. She was familiar with her husband's approach and was well versed in what his business was. She kept the conversation going by saying, "She's Joie, dear" and gave him a wink. I liked her style of keeping things light. Gino never spoke within that short interaction but I could tell something didn't sit right with him. It was in his eyes and written in the look of his face. I had been with him long enough to notice. He played it cool though. For appearances sake, he kept up with the conversation and tried his hardest not to let on that something was wrong. As we all chatted in that small room, people took notice. The other mob heads and wives would look in the room and were taken a bit by surprise because they never expected me and Gino to be interacting with one of the Patriarchs of the Mafia. They never attempted to cross that line and associate with Santo because many of them didn't want to be on his radar. Something about me and Gino stuck out to him though and he made it known we were in his good graces. The short time we spent in that room was enough to let others know we were established and at the top of the food chain compared to them.

Saying our goodbyes, I stood and shook Josie's hand. I thanked her for her time and for being such a wonderful person to meet. She gave me her number and told me to call her anytime. I actually looked forward to speaking with her soon. I turned to say goodbye to Santo and he shook my hand. He kissed it like a gentleman and said he hoped to hear from us again. For some reason, I knew we were going to be contact very soon.

Returning home from the wake, I noticed Gino was very quiet. He wasn't speaking much and went straight to the liquor cabinet. He poured himself a drink of Vino and took the bottle in to his study. I wanted to check on him but I felt it best to give him some space. I had known at the wake that he wasn't his normal self. Something was truly bothering him. In the distance, I heard our house phone ringing. Picking up the phone by the fourth ring, I said hello. To my surprise, there was a familiar voice on the other end. "Hello Joie, this is Santo. Don't say my name out loud and stay very calm. Are you busy right now?" his voice from the other end of the phone sounded so comforting to me in that moment. "No I'm not busy," I replied. I was a little nervous because of how he came on the line. I wasn't sure at first how to handle the call but I played it off as best as I could. "Joie, there's a little café on 163rd Street in Miami. I would like for you to meet me there in about an hour. Is this possible?" I was in shock. Santo was calling and asking to meet me, not Gino. I was a little suspicious at first but I agreed to the meeting. I was excited more than anything for the opportunity to sit down again with a man that had such great power. I went and freshened myself up a bit and then checked on Gino. His back was to me but I could see he was about halfway in to the bottle so I was pretty sure he wasn't going anywhere soon. I grabbed my keys and headed out the door, unaware of what I was walking in to but still ready for anything.

Sitting in the café on 163rd Street, I looked around at the waitresses. It brought fond memories of my time working in the restaurant with Dee Dee. I had come so far from those days. I never thought I would have truly made it out of there since my plans were on school and nursing. Here I was now on a completely different path. The choices in our lives truly do alter the outcome. As the waitress took my order for a cup of coffee and a muffin, I turned my attention to the windows that looked out on the street. I was observant of my surroundings because those I worked for and all that I dabbled in myself. It was my way of never having my guard down. I spotted an old black Galaxy 500 pull up in front of the small café, as the driver came around to the passenger door I knew before he opened it who was going to step out. Everything about Santo screamed class act. No one could hold water to him and his presence. He carried himself so well for a man of such power. He was neither loud nor obnoxious like the other bosses. He was quiet, he kept his composure at all times and seemed very genuine in all that he did and said. He never boasted or bragged about anything he had, which believe me he had more than anyone I knew. He was honestly a *"down to earth type"* of man. I really did admire him for those reasons and more. As Santo took his seat across from me, I felt my heart race a little and my face blush.

"Good evening Joie. I'm so glad you could make it," he said. I smiled and responded by saying, "When a man of your stature asks so eloquently for my presence I just can't resist." I noticed his smile grow across his face. "I like your spunk Joie. I have heard many things about you. From what I see right now most of it must be true." "Well, it depends on what you heard and who from," I teased. In the Mafia, many people like to make stories up. It's a way of keeping others on their toes. Some of what you would hear is as phony as the people who created the stories. But still, under everything there is always a small line of truth. "I hear from the streets that you're out there taking risks and running things. I hear that Gino lets you do the dirty work and takes the credit. That's not right Joie" he said to me. "Yes, it's true. I'm a soldier. I do what is necessary to keep the boss happy." I replied but felt a bit of anger because I knew what he was saying

151

was truthful. I was busting ass and Gino was getting credit. No matter how far I may come, I knew it was still a man's world. "Joie, I'd like to offer you an opportunity. I want you to work for me. You can keep the job you have with the Old Man and Gino because I wouldn't want you to completely turn your back on those that have been there for you. I just want to offer you the chance to have your own for a change. I know Gino is providing for you. A woman like you should be well off. She should never have to ask or need for anything. I would like to put you on my payroll in exchange for small favors, nothing that you haven't already done before or that would risk too much." "You're offering me a job?" I asked. "Exactly. I want you to discreetly work for me. This would be an arrangement strictly between us. No one, not even Gino, needs to know. I have a home in the Miami area. I feel that there is a great deal of money that can be made out here. What Hyman Larner is doing right now is very small time compared to what can really be accomplished. With my pull from New York, I want to organize things a bit better and make them more main stream. I would like you to help me," he said. "What would I need to do?" I asked. If what Hyman Larner was doing was only the tip of the iceberg then I definitely wanted in to where it was going to be most lucrative. Money and power were what was important. I wanted to be able to make it on my own without handouts and standing in someone else's shadow. "All I need you to do is be my eyes and ears when I can't be around. Let me know what's going on in a quiet and discreet way. In return, I plan to place you on my payroll. A woman like you should be paid and well off. She is a true jewel and not to be treated like scraps will satisfy her. I respect you Joie. I think we could have a very good working relationship." Everything he said made so much sense to me. If all I had to do was tell him what was going on and not even break a nail in the process then I was in. I was starting to have the business mind frame. Whatever made money was the smart choice and the clear option to choose. Whatever lost money was something I stayed away from. This business proposal from Santo was definitely a money maker. Many other mafia soldiers would have jumped at the chance that he presented without considering any consequences. Why should I let the boys have all the fun? I go for what I want in life. "I would be honored to work for you," I said. The words were so honest when I spoke them that even Santo believed in me. For some reason within that instant, I felt I could trust him too. He was the strong, quiet type but his intelligence and genuine nature spoke volumes for him.

For the next few months, Santo and I began to form a close knit bond. I would go and do my usual routines for Gino and in between I would find time to meet with Santo. We would meet at the café on 163rd Street or sometimes we would even meet up at movie theatres to exchange information. Santo was always very discreet. During our meetings, I informed him of the comings and goings of Hyman Larner and the others. If anyone spotted us, no one ever said anything directly to me or Santo. I think it was out of fear no one came forward and questioned me since it was well known how Santo was connected. It wasn't until Santo fell ill for the first time that our relationship was brought to light by Hyman Larner.

Gino and I were called to visit The Old Man. He had just purchased another condo in Miami. This one may have been my favorite. It was a beautiful wrap around condominium with beige marble floors, mirrors on the walls and a circular bar with swivel chairs that was located close to a wall of glass that looked out over the ocean. The lights were dim over the bar to create the perfect ambiance. Gino and I were served cocktails and enjoyed them as we looked around. Hyman entered the room and asked us to have a seat on the tan leather couches that were placed so eloquently in the sunken living room. Everything was so modern. Hyman took his seat on the matching couch and welcomed us to his new place. Gino thanked him for his courtesy and for having us over. With the Mafia, everything is just for appearances. This meeting called by Larner was no different.

"Thank you both so much for coming here today," the Old Man said and took a sip of his Cognac. "Now I need to get down straight to business. As you both are aware, Santo was in Tampa. Today, he was placed in the hospital due to illness. His wife is at his side keeping vigil. As a good show of face, we need to move on this and bring some money over to his wife and family. It's a token of loyalty and respect," the Old Man said. The Mafia code was to provide for the family of those that is in power or of a fallen foot soldier. It was respect. It was *"famiglia prendersi cura della famiglia"* meaning family taking care of family. "I'll be more than honored to do that as a favor for you," said Gino. He was quick to volunteer for anything Hyman Larner needed done. "Though I appreciate your offer Gino, this is something Joie needs to do," he said. Gino's face was one of pure shock. "Why her?" he asked puzzled. "Why not her? She knows Santo personally. She and his wife are friends. She is exactly who needs to be there for us since she's a friendly face," Larner said straight at me. Never once did I flinch or seem bothered by his statement. The truth was I was Santo's liaison. I let him know what was going on and who was coming to town. Nothing was withheld from him. We had been meeting at the movies, coffee houses, and small hotels in the Miami area. Even cafeterias and hospitals were used as covers. From our meetings, I could feel a bond grow between

155

Santo and I. Gino shot a piercing look at the side of my face and I still was unmoved. "Of course Hyman, it will be my pleasure to take care of that for you." As I spoke I could feel the anger growing from Gino's end of the couch but he didn't dare allow it to surface in front of the Old Man. Gino never anticipated I would one day step out in to the front lines before him. Hyman knew all too well and could sense my readiness. Hyman was fully aware that I was already doing most of the work for Gino anyway. Part of me knew that this was more than just a friendly drop off. I truly feel it was a test of my loyalty as well. The Old Man handed me an envelope that contained five thousand dollars and first class plane ticket. He told me Santo was taken to Tampa General Hospital and everything else I needed would be inside the envelope. "When do you want me to leave?" I asked. "Right away," said Larner. I nodded my head and gave Gino a glance. He turned his head as if he was looking out at the view of the ocean. I took the envelope and ticket and went home to pack. I knew in that moment Gino felt he was out done by me. I knew it was something that I would probably hear about one way or another. I didn't really care. I had a job to do. Like any other good employee, I was trying to stay on the good side of the boss to be able to move up the totem pole. This was a perfect way to do it. Hyman Larner may have been testing me, but I was still grateful because I could demonstrate to both him and Santo I can get the job done. I was on my way without a blink of the eye.

Arriving at the hospital, I spotted Josie and the family speaking to a doctor. I didn't want to be rude so I poked around the floor until I found Santo. He was lying in a bed with all kinds of machines hooked up to him. The curtains were drawn and he looked pale. "How are ya doing Pop?" I asked as I got closer to the foot of his bed. I started calling him Pop as my own personal nickname and joke between us. "I've had better days but I've also had worse. Did you see Josie outside?" he asked. Even through his illness, he was concerned with his wife's well being. He truly was a gentleman. "Yeah, I saw her Pop. She was with the doctor. I came here for two reasons. I needed to check up on you. I heard you were sick and I had to see it for myself. I didn't think Superman got ill," I teased him. He let out a chuckle. "Well you forgot even he has his own weakness, Kryptonite. So what's the other reason you're here?" "The Old Man sent me," I said and took the envelope out and placed it on his side table. Santo glanced over at the envelope and back at me. "So he's not as dumb as thought he was. That's good to know. Where do we stand at this moment?" he asked. "All he knows right now is that I am friend of you and your wife. He asked me to bring the money to show respect to you," I replied. "Tell him I accept this token and thank him from me. Now can you do me a favor?" he said with such a soft voice. "Anything for you, Pop. What do you need?" "Take Josie for something good to eat. She has been at my side all day. This hospital food is shit. Make sure she's taken care of," he said. "Of course," I smiled in reply. The love shared between the two of them was actually refreshing to watch. It gave me a bit of hope for the World. "Get some rest Santo. I'll take care of your wife," I promised. Stepping outside of the room, I saw that Josie was done with the doctor. I sat beside her and said, "I know you're here for him but you need your strength. Come on; let's go get something to eat. He's worried about you." She took my hand and said "Thank you Joie." Josie and I left the Mafia business alone that day. We were simply two women going for a meal, a drink and some girl time.

Josie and I ended up at an Italian restaurant and placed our drink orders first. Who could resist a good glass of red wine? After the waiter came back with our drinks, Josie opened up a bit to me. "He's sick," she said. "I know but you have to stay strong for him. He will be better soon," I tried my best to be comforting. "Not this time. He's very ill. The doctors are saying its Angina. I don't have the heart to tell him." "Oh my god Josie, I'm so sorry. Did they tell you anything else?" I asked. What I was hearing was both very shocking and very sad to me because I had grown so close to

Santo. "You know doctors. They say a lot and most of which gets blocked out as soon as they mention a horrible disease." I shot her a quick glance not realizing Santo was that sick I was caught off guard. "I know to other people my husband might be seen as a bad person, but to me he's everything. He's my life and love," she said with tears in her eyes. "Don't worry about what those bastards may think. He's your husband Josie. That's all they should care about. You stand beside him and see him through everything. You're a strong woman and he's going to need that. Who gives a shit about some of these low lives out there! Most of them couldn't even come close to a piece of gum on his shoes. Your husband is a good man Josie. Remember that." "Thank you Joie for being a good friend to me. It means a lot to me. Arriving back in Miami to report to Hyman Larner, I wasn't sure what to expect but I knew I had accomplished the job he sent me out to complete. Santo had the envelope of money for his family and Josie had a sympathetic ear to listen to her. All in all, it was a job well done. The Old Man was very pleased and knew where my loyalty stood or so he thought. I still knew I had another man yet to answer to, Gino.

# Joie Miami

## Chapter Eleven:  The Beginning of the End

Shortly after proving myself to The Old Man and Santo my reputation began to grow.  It was 1987 and my name was being spoken on the streets like a celebrity and everyone wanted a piece of Joie.  Restaurant and shop owners began putting my bills "on the house."  News stations and magazines began contacting me for articles because of stories of a "Lady Mafia" and a "Femme Fatale" that were being told.  Television and radio talk shows were mentioning my name and showing my face.  I even made an appearance on multiple outlets.  I was no longer living in Gino's shadow.  The spotlight was focusing on me.  I was calling the shots and was a sensation in their eyes because I was a woman with power and wasn't taking any prisoners.  I had all the superficial signs of status thanks to Santo and was earning more money and respect on my own then I was ever given by Gino. Life couldn't have gotten any better for me and Nikki, who was now fourteen years old.  But as the saying goes, "that which is given can be easily taken away."

At the height of my popularity, things began to crumble slowly around me at home. There was a shift in Gino's behavior which caused tension between us. Perhaps he felt he was being put out to pasture? His jealousy was no longer hidden and our home was no longer happy. He began to drink more often and loose himself to the dark side. His mental and physical healths were deteriorating slowly. He even lost his zest for life. He would sit at home with the drapes all drawn closed and in the dark. Whenever I attempted to talk to him all I would see was the fiery tip of his cigarette.

Soon, my life felt reminiscent of my childhood. Gino's drinking brought out the worst in him. I began feeling like I traded my drunken and abusive father for an equally mean and hateful lover. It was like I exchanged one prison for another. Gino was belligerent and nasty towards me. Nikki was impacted the most from his actions because he was the only father she ever knew. She truly loved him but couldn't stand to be around him when he was drunk. I was so conditioned by my father's abuse that I was just waiting for the day I would have to put a bullet in Gino for daring to put his hands on me. I couldn't take it anymore and finally left him. I got an apartment for Nikki and myself. To save face, Gino fronted all the bills but only doled out just enough for us to get by; everything else was coming from my pocket. I had some cash saved up but it wouldn't be long before I burned through it all. I couldn't go to Hyman Larner for assistance because Gino didn't want word to get out of our crumbling home life. For all purposes he wanted things to look like we were still together. So I turned to the one man that I knew would help me. I visited Santo. I had gone to him several times before for Gene. Never did he hesitate. He always ensured I had exactly what I came for. I knew if I told him I was in need he would take care of me.

"Joie, please come in. It's so nice to see you," Santo's wife, Josie, opened the door. Josie was always so welcoming with her southern comfort. She led me to the living room and told me to have a seat. "I'll go find my husband," she said and was off to look for him. I adored their home. It gave off that feeling of love and was so inviting.

"Joie, welcome," Santo said as he entered the room. "How are you?" "I'm good Pop. How are you feeling?" I asked. I had heard his health was starting to take a turn for the worse. "Some days I'm good. Some days I'm not so good," he said. "Well you still look great Pop," I said trying to be nice. In all honesty, he looked a bit pale and kind of fragile. To see a man of such power being broken down due to bad health was like watching a building of grand stature slowly crumble. It was heart breaking.

"So what brings you by to see me?" he asked. "Well, I'm in need of some money." I said feeling a bit embarrassed. "Gene okay?" he asked. "Yeah Pop, but it's not for Gino. I'm in a situation and it would help me greatly," I watched as his eyes looked over me as if trying to read me. "I'll pay it back to you if you want," I told him. I didn't want to come across as if I was begging. "Joie, you don't have to pay me back. You've done a lot for me and my family. I appreciate your loyalty. Of course, I'll help you," Santo said. He went over to a desk in the room and opened a drawer. Inside was where he kept some of his money. He came beside me and sat down. "Here, take this envelope. I have something else I want to give you too," he said. He put his hand out and there was a small black box. "Santo, thank you. I don't need anything else," I said. "Take it. It's a small token of my appreciation to you," his eyes looked at me lovingly like a father. I took the box and opened it up. Inside was a beautiful pair of diamond post earrings. "Oh Santo they're gorgeous. Thank you." I gave him a hug. In a way, I believe he already knew that Gino and I separated without having to tell him. He took my hand and said, "Joie, don't worry. Everything is going to be fine. I have to go and see this doctor soon. When I come back to town we'll talk more. I'll make sure you and your daughter are well provided for." In that moment, I knew what it must have been like to feel a father's love. "I don't know how to thank you enough Santo," I said. I didn't like showing too much emotion but he could see the tears I was fighting back. I left Santo's home that day and felt comforted. Sadly, it was the last time I ever saw Santo again. The day after I saw him, Santo was scheduled to go for surgery. He died on the operating table. When word made its way to me I was in total shock. The man I trusted and highly respected was gone forever. That's when I realized the earrings were really his parting gift for me. I knew any hope for me and Nikki was going to slim to none now. I had given Gino and the Mafia the best years of my life. I had to find a different way to survive.

A few months after Santo's passing, Nikki went to stay with Gino for a weekend. She understood that I felt he was making my life a living hell, but she refused to turn her back on him. I would never make her choose between us. I was a ruthless bitch in the streets but when it came to my child I wanted what was in her best interest. I went over to Gino's to pick her up. Gino was out in the yard. He came in the house and his arm was swollen. "What happened to you?" I asked. "I don't know. I must have banged it outside," he said. Nikki took one look at his arm and freaked out. "Dad, we've got to get you to a doctor. You need to have it looked at. It's pretty bad," she said. Gino wouldn't listen to her. "I'm not going to a doctor." His objection was painful for her to hear. "Please Dad. It's for your own good," she begged. "I said no." I knew how hard headed Gino could be and understood there was no point in arguing with him. "I'll get some ice," I said trying to be the mediator between them. "Don't worry about it. It's nothing," Gino replied. Since we separated, he kept a distance between us. His refusal to the ice pack was just another way of keeping the walls up. "Fine. Come on Nikki. Let's get going. He says he's fine, then he's fine," I was done trying to debate with him. Truthfully, the last year between us and the death of Santo took a lot out of me. Nikki's eyes were stuck on Gino and his swollen arm as we left the house. My daughter's compassion and mercy for this man was limitless. In the car on the way home he was all she thought about. "Ma, we got to get him to a doctor. I don't like how he's looking. Something isn't right. I can feel it in my gut." I had never heard her so determined. "Okay, I'll talk to him. I'll see what I can do," I had to agree with her. He really didn't look too good. I also knew when a woman's intuition starts talking you better listen.

Nikki went to school with children whose parents were all professionals. One of her classmate's had a father that was a doctor. She spoke with him about her father's sudden swollen arm and how he's been looking. He told her when Gino was ready he would see him and keep it completely confidential. Nikki knew he would never make an appointment

165

on his own so she set everything up for him to be seen at the Jackson Memorial Hospital. Gino knew how persistent she was and eventually he caved in and agreed. To ensure he went, Nikki had me drive them both. Gene was subjected to a battery of tests and x-rays. We all went together to the follow up appointment to hear the results and that's when our world came to a crashing halt.

Sitting in the doctor's office, Nikki held her father's hand. She knew there was something going on but she couldn't put her finger on it. I was there for moral support. The doctor entered the room with a look upon his face that read like an open book. We all knew something serious was about to go down. Before he spoke, he placed the x-rays Gino previously had taken up on a screen. From working as a nurse's assistant when I was younger, I scanned the film out of habit and knew before he opened his mouth what he was about to say. Nikki was so intuitive she turned to the doctor and said, "My father has two tumors. Am I correct?" Gino sat and looked lost for a moment. The doctor shook his head in agreement. "Mr. Talarico, after reviewing the test results as well as the x-rays we have found that you have a collapsed lung. In addition, you do in fact have two tumors. It appears that you have entered Stage Four Lung Cancer. There are treatments for it which could give you a year, perhaps a little more time.

166

Without being treated, you may have six months left. I know that this is overwhelming news to you all. I am deeply sorry. If you decide that you would like to attempt the radiation therapy, I will have to refer you to an Oncologist right away. I really am sorry Mr. Talarico." We all sat silently for a minute. Gino stood up and walked out of the room without speaking. Nikki and I thanked the doctor for helping us and told him we would be in touch. "Ladies, he needs to be admitted to the hospital as soon as possible so we can get his treatments started. I really am so very sorry to have to deliver such disturbing news to you."

When we got in to the car Gino had a puzzled look on his face. "Nikki, what did he mean? I don't understand," he said to her with a look begging to hear something different. She placed her hand on his arm gently and said, "Dad, you have terminal cancer. We have to follow the doctor's orders now and get you checked in to the hospital." "What are you talking about?" he said in denial. "Gino, you're sick. There's no way around this one," I said to him. Nikki put her head down in the backseat and began sobbing. "I'm not sick. I'm fine. Take me home now," he said. He simply refused to accept what was being told to him. "Dad you have to go to the hospital now!" Nikki screamed at him. He knew his battle was finally lost. He didn't have any more strength to argue. Within twenty four hours of starting chemotherapy, his appearance completely changed. His complexion was soured and his eyes had a yellow haze over them. His body wasn't accepting the treatments well. He was dying slowly before our eyes. Nikki began grieving for the only man she ever knew as a father.

Word of his illness began to circulate and soon I was receiving phone calls from The Old Man, Sal Bastone and Wayne Redoway. Wayne was one of Gino's best friends from working the boats and wanted to pay respects. Gino didn't have insurance. Working for the Mafia came with certain benefits but health insurance and a 401K were definitely not a part of them. They all came to the hospital to see him during one of his treatments. The Old Man pulled me aside, "Joie, we're going to pay all the bills here. Don't worry about nothing. Just focus on Gene and getting him settled." It was Larner's way of telling me it was time for me to focus on his funeral arrangements. We all knew and accepted it wasn't going to be long before we would have to say our goodbyes to him. I had found the name of a lawyer, Mr. Levy, which the Mafia frequently used when contracts and wills needed to be drawn up. I knew I had to start getting all of Gino's final affairs in order by myself. Gino wasn't in his right mind and his family was never really there for him.

"Have you contacted Gene's son?" his friend Wayne asked me. "Why would I? In the fourteen years Gino and I have been together only once has he come to see his father," I replied with a bit of shock in my voice. "He's still his father. This is something that he needs to know," he said with a point blank expression on his face. "Yeah alright. I'll take care of it," I said trying to brush off the uncomfortable feeling I had over the topic at hand. "I know you will Joie. Don't worry about it." I wasn't worried about it at all. In all the years that Gino and I spent together, my daughter was the only child that was ever at his constant side. Even as he was ailing with cancer, my daughter held his head as he vomited from treatments and bathed him in the hospital because the nurses were doing a half assed job. She even made sure he had food since the hospital's menu was more like bird food. An extra bed was placed in his room just for Nikki to sleep on. She was going to see him through his battle with cancer all the way to the end. Gino did what he could to be an active role in his son's life by sending money to his child's mother but she never attempted to respond to his efforts. I'm sure they appreciated the money he sent to provide a life for his son. It was only during the Holidays when Gene received card. Of course they knew they would receive money in return. Gene Jr.'s mother was also on the money bandwagon since he never married her. Why should I make an effort for them to know about his death when they never cared about his life? As far as I was concerned, Nikki and I were his family and we were taking care of things for him. I kept my feelings and emotions on the topic to myself though. I knew it wouldn't be wise to bring it up while in the hospital.

It didn't take long for the vultures to show up on my front door. Gino's son and his Uncle appeared one day at our home. A friend of Hyman Larner contacted them behind my back and let them know about Gene's illness. While Gino was in the hospital, I would stay at the house and make sure the bills were getting paid and the cleaning and lawn were kept up. I heard the knock and opened the door. If I would have known ahead of time that they were there to rip everything out from under my feet I never would have opened the door.

"Can I help you?" I said. It was Gene Jr. and his Uncle. "I'm looking for my father Gino," he said. "Your father's at the Jackson Memorial Hospital receiving radiation therapy. He'll be home in a couple days if you want to see him," I felt like I wanted to choke saying those words to his son. The idea of someone seeing a man when he is about to die instead of visiting when he is full of life still didn't sit too well with me. "Thank you. We'll be back to see him soon," Gene Jr. said and with that he was gone. A nagging feeling in the pit of my stomach was telling me there was more to come and I knew I had to brace myself. Later on that day, I went to the hospital to bring Gino his small portable television. The Chicago Bears were playing and he never missed a game. I knew he wouldn't want to start now. Entering in the room, I saw Nikki's bed was empty. She must have gone out to get something for them to eat. I found a place for the television and as I set it up I looked over at Gino.

"Your son came to the house today," I mentioned casually. I didn't want to stress him out too much. "Oh yeah," he said. The treatments were strong and left him disoriented sometimes. "How's he looking?" he asked. "He looks like you Gino," I said. "Poor bastard," he replied. At least I knew his sense of humor was still in a good place. "He wants to see you soon. I told him to visit after your treatments at the house to give you both some privacy." "Yeah. That's good. Did you contact the lawyer?" he asked. "I got a hold of him. We have to go and see Mr. Levy on Thursday. He needs you to sign off on some paperwork. You think you can handle that?" He had gotten very weak and fragile from everything his body was going through. Sometimes when he was home just standing in the yard was too much for him. "I'll be there. It needs to be done," he said. Nikki had come back. She had some food with her. Even I was happy to see that they weren't eating the shit the hospital was trying to push off as edible.

Gene Jr. and his Uncle returned Thursday morning bright and early. I had no idea that Gino contacted them by phone and asked them to be there. Nikki was in the kitchen fixing breakfast for her father. She never heard the knock on the front door. I escorted them to the living room where Gino was sitting and looking at the newspaper. "Hi Dad, it's been a long time," Gene Jr. said as he stepped in to the room. Hearing him say the word "Dad" made my stomach clench. I knew it would be a stab to Nikki's heart hearing anyone else call Gino "Dad" since she had been with him so long. Gene Jr. took a seat on the couch by his father. His Uncle sat in a chair close to the window. You could tell he was uncomfortable from the uneasy silence about him.

"Okay Dad, I've got some breakfast here for you. The doctor told me you have to eat healthy to keep up your strength," Nikki said as she entered the room. "Oh, I'm sorry I didn't know Gene Jr. was here," she looked at the men in surprise. "Nikki can you excuse us, please," Gino said. For the first time in her life, he made my daughter feel like she didn't belong. I felt my child's pain and watched as she left the room. I followed behind her to comfort her. Everything was overwhelming and very hard to swallow, even for me. "Ma, what the hell was that?" she said to me. "I had to leave the room because of *his son*. That's *my* Dad too. I love him more than that man ever could. I have been with him every step of the way. He raised me and I had to leave the room so he could talk to *his son*? Where was his son when he needed the appointments made or someone there for him through his treatments?" "I know honey. I don't understand it but we got to keep strong right now," I told her. "Nikki and Joie we're ready to go," said Gene Jr. "What do you mean we?" I said confused. "My father has asked for me to join him at the lawyers," he said with ice in his tones. "What?" I couldn't believe what I heard. I went back in to the living room and confronted Gino. "You told your son he could come to the lawyers with us?" I said without caring whether the others heard or not. "Yeah, I did. I want him there. This shouldn't be a problem," he said to me. It was like someone else programmed his response to me. "Fine, Gino. I'll get the car ready," I said with anger building up inside of me. Nikki was just as shocked and confused as I was. She followed me to the car asking questions all along the way. "What the hell is going on? Ma, I don't get this. What is he thinking right now?" "I don't know Nikki. Let's just get to the lawyers office and take it from there," was all I could reply to her. As sure as I knew blood ran through my veins, I knew Nikki and I were about to get fucked over. I was doing all I could to give Gino the benefit of the doubt, but I had tingles all through my body. My female intuition was in overdrive. I could feel something just was not right. Pulling the car in the front of the house, I was waiting for Gino to get in the car. "My father will be riding with us," Gene Jr. said. "We'll follow close behind you." It became clear to me now that this was going to be a set up. Working for the Mafia long enough, I knew bullshit a mile away. Gene Jr. was trying to run game on his sick father and Gino was eating it up. The long lost son routine was getting old real quickly. Nikki was just as irritated as I was. She wasn't slow by any means and knew Gene Jr. was playing his cards well.

At the lawyers, Gino sat in front and I was right next to him. I'd be damned if I gave Gene Jr. the opportunity to chime in or stake claim to anything that I helped Gino to build. Nikki sat on my right with Gene Jr. on his father's left. "Thank you all for coming here today," Mr. Levy said looking around the room at all of us. "As I can imagine handling the Last Will and Testament of Mr. Talarico, as well as his estate is going to be hard. Some tough decisions have to be made though. We need to make sure everything gets handled exactly to Mr. Talarico's final wishes. I know this is a bit much right now, especially with your health not being one hundred percent but I assure you it's for the best interest of all parties involved," the lawyer was rattling off. As that man spoke, I could feel the tension in the room begin to grow. "I want to make sure my son is taken care of," Gino said. I almost gave myself whiplash with how fast I turned my head. "*Your son?* What about me and Nikki?" "What about you? You have each other. Gene Jr. is my blood. He's my son. I've gotta look out for him," he said. It was like a slap in both of mine and my daughter's face. It was the explosion in my brain that I was waiting for all day. I knew something shady was going on and here it was. I just couldn't believe what I was hearing and neither could Nikki. Nikki and I were being left out in the cold. "Are you serious Dad?" Nikki yelled. Before I did something I would have regretted in the lawyer's office, I stood up and stormed out. Nikki grabbed her stuff. "I can't believe you would do this to us. I looked up to you as a father," she said. "He's not your father," Gene Jr. said as if to add insult to injury, "he's mine." The tears shot out of Nikki's eyes and she left the office hysterical. I watched as she ran to the car with her hands on her face to hide her emotions. Pure hatred was in the pit of my belly and I was ready to unleash it. Gino came running out of the office behind her. "Nikki! Nikki wait!" He had tears of his own. For the first time ever, I saw him cry. "Joie, please let's not leave things like this," he begged. "You sonuvabitch. I gave you the best years of my fuckin' life. Nikki loved you with every inch of her heart. She wiped the vomit off of your fuckin' face and washed your ass in the hospital and this is how you repay us!" "He's my son!" Gino screamed. I couldn't control my anger anymore. I spit in his face. "Fuck you and your son! You're so fuckin' blind and don't see he's only here for what he can get from your death! He doesn't give a shit about you. My daughter was with you every day since she was two years old. You treat a stranger better than her? You treat me like trash! I hate you, you bastard!" I didn't give a damn about anyone watching. I didn't give a damn about his medical condition. I hoped and prayed Gino would have dropped dead in the street before walking back in that office to sign any documents that gave anything to his son. How dare he let this motherfucker come in and take everything that belonged to me and my child! Gene Jr. came out and got between us. "Joie, I can understand you're upset but family sticks together." "Fuck you and your family!" I spit on his shoes and turned my back to them. "Joie! Come back Joie!" Gino yelled behind me. I didn't dare turn around to look at him. I was concentrated on getting to my daughter- *my family.* Nikki was inconsolable in the car. She was broken down. As I started up the car Gene Jr. came knocking on the window. I flipped him off and threw the car in reverse. I spotted Gino crying like a baby in the grass in front of the office building. It was a big difference from the cool and subdued nature he displayed all those years ago when we first met. I made sure to give him the finger too. He knew I was done with him and nothing he could say would change that. I had never dared to disrespect him in any way when we were together but this was too damn much to take in.

With massive anger balling up in my stomach again, I drove over to Gino's house. Nikki didn't say a word the entire time we were in the car until we pulled up in the drive way and I told her to get out of the car. "Why are we here Ma?" she asked. "We're claiming what's ours right now!" I told her. I opened the door and gave her instructions to go in to Gino's bedroom and grab every piece of jewelry she could find. While she did that I knew where he had some money stashed and planned to wipe it out. I was smart and wanted to make sure Gene felt the same betrayal I did so I also grabbed the ledger he kept his secrets in. Time was running out, I knew better then to stay too long in the house. They would probably be back any time soon and I didn't plan to be there when they arrived. I grabbed whatever I could. Nikki came from the bedroom with a box full of jewelry that belonged to Gino. We didn't have time to take anything else. I had hoped I could come back and do a clean sweep of some more items and scoop up what was mine. I had taken most of my stuff when I got the apartment but there were still some things I left behind. "Come on let's go. Let's get out of here before those bastards return!" I told Nikki and we headed towards the door. Pulling out of the driveway and heading up the street, I spotted Gino's car in my rearview mirror. A smirk went across my face just thinking that they were about to see what happens when Nikki and I stick together.

For days following the incident at the lawyers, Gino would call my home phone. I knew he wanted to apologize but there was nothing he could say to erase the damage he had done. Gene Jr. even had the audacity to call once too. He told me that his father was selling the house and because my name was on the documents they needed me to sign off on some paperwork. I told him to go fuck himself and hung up on him. I heard through the grapevine Gene Jr. was cleaning everything out of there because he was taking Gino back to Chicago to spend his remaining days there. His family swarmed in like locusts and destroyed everything we had left. They were money hungry bastards and wanted to squeeze every dime they could from him. Beds, tables, rugs, pictures of a life we lived were all being sold or boxed up. This is what Gino reduced our lives to, allowing strangers to sift through our memories. I couldn't believe everything had been ripped right out from under me. Fourteen years of dedication to a man was all for nothing. He used to tell me, "Don't worry, when I die you and Nikki will be well taken care of." Now I see what he meant- that motherfucker!

With no money to come my way from Gino's estate, I knew I had to get my head back in the game. I needed to pull some jobs to make money so me and Nikki could survive. I knew all the ins and outs from running things for Gino so I hoped it wouldn't be an issue to get connected. I was wrong. I sat down and made a list of the people that Gene and I associated with. Everyone from The Old Man to Sal Bastone was on it. I began calling people to ask for help. I wasn't looking for handouts. I was looking for work. I had hoped my years of dedicated service in the Mafia as a liaison would mean something, anything. It turned out it all meant shit. One by one they all turned me down. I was fed excuses and lies as to why they couldn't do anything for me. The Old Man even said he wanted nothing to do with me because of what happened between me and Gino. Jews were supposed to be trustworthy. They would sell a deal on an honorable handshake. I did more for that bastard then just shake his hand and after everything was done and all I witnessed; after all the secrets I kept and the parties I planned; I was left out in the cold as a forgotten soldier. The men I trusted and risked going to prison for had turned their backs on me and left me stranded. A woman once again had no place at their table. Furious over this betrayal, I did something I never thought I would ever do. I stole from my own kind and broke my code of loyalty. Those dumb fucks had forgotten I was the one that cleaned their apartments and homes. I had keys to several of Hyman Larner's apartments he used for hosting guests like Noriega and storage facilities and knew how to be low key without anyone being the wiser. The training I got from the Mafia helped me in my thefts. Those motherfuckers were so egotistical they never would have assumed a woman would be so bold. Chandeliers, tennis equipment, luggage and anything else I felt I could make a good buck off of I took right out from underneath them and no one assumed it was me. I didn't give a fuck. I had given so much to the Mafia. It was time I took back what I wanted. I refused to go back to the deprived lifestyle my parents raised me in. I had come so far to turn around and back track now. I knew the items I took would buy me some time but the cash flow I was looking for wasn't going to come from stealing. The only thing I had left to gain monetarily from was information and the only people who would buy it were the ones I worked hard to hide it from, the Feds.

Joie Miami

## Chapter Twelve:  Breaking the Code of Silence

It was November 1989 and right before Thanksgiving, Nikki and I began struggling in our new lives.  We weren't used to living like normal people.  I had taken on three jobs to make bills and couldn't stand sliding backwards.  We had lived high on the hog for so long that we didn't know how to function scraping money together.  I couldn't continue living like this.  I knew that the only real way to dig myself out of the mess I was in was by selling the one valuable thing I had left- information.

I sat at my kitchen table and put the phonebook in front of me to find the number I was looking for.  It was for the Federal Bureau of Investigations Building located off of 167th Street in Miami.  With a deep breath in my lungs and hatred in my blood for what had been done to me and my daughter, I picked up the phone and dialed the number.  A man's voice came on the line.  I couldn't turn back now I thought and began to speak.

"My name is Joie Talarico. I think I can be of some help to you. I've been involved with gentlemen like Gino Talarico, Joseph DeVida, Hyman Larner, and Sal Bastone. If you need more names I'll be glad to give them to you." "Just a moment, please. I'll connect you with an agent that can further assist you," he said. My heart was pounding out of my chest. I had shivers of dread going through me. My mind was going crazy. *What am I doing? I should hang up! Fuck it! If the Mob had played fair and by their rules, I never would have been making this call. I had no choice.*

"Hello, Mrs. Talarico," I heard come from the phone. It was another man's voice. "I'm agent, Dean Hughes. I'd like to set up a meeting with you if that's possible," he said. "That's why I'm on the phone calling you," I said with cockiness in my voice.

"Great. Would it be possible for me to come over to your home and sit down face to face this evening?" "Sure, I'll be waiting on you," I responded and still couldn't believe what came out of my mouth.

"Okay, can I have your address?" he asked. I started laughing. "What's so funny?" he inquired. "I thought you could trace everything," I said. "Sure let me give you my address."

Exactly twenty minutes passed before building security called to tell me that a Mr. Dean Hughes was at the gate waiting for me. I told the guard to let him through and soon I heard the familiar sound of my door bell ringing. A tall, balding Midwesterner was at my door identifying himself as a federal agent. He was wearing a dark blue suit and carrying a brown accordion folder tied together with a red string and knotted. He entered my home and to my surprise there was another man behind him. "Gee, if I would have known we were having additional company I would have made cookies," I teased. They were polite and complimented my home but the other man never introduced himself to me. We all sat around the coffee table in the living room. Hughes opened his folder and began to take out a stack of photographs.

"Mrs. Talarico, I'm going to show you some pictures. Do you think you can identify the people in them?" he asked. "Sure, I'll give it a try," I said.

"Do you know this man?" he asked pointing to a photo of a very familiar face. "I might," I said. "Okay, do you know this man?" he asked pointing to another photo. "Maybe I do," I responded. Hughes laughed and looked at his companion. "What do you mean 'maybe'?" his voice was more insistent but he was smiling.

"Well, how much money do you have?" I asked him. The other man shot Hughes a look. "How much are we talking about here?" Hughes inquired. "I have to think about since it depends on how much information you want," I said with a point blank look on my face. "So gentleman," I said, "How much information are you looking for?" "Whatever you want. Just write down the amount on a piece of paper. Now if you can answer my next question, I'll see to it that the amount you write down is what you get paid. Have we got a deal?" Both men were staring straight at me. "Deal," I said.

"Do you know who this man is?" he said holding up a photograph. I figured it was time to prove myself to them and let them know I wasn't some kind of crack pot. "Yes, it's Vinnie Ruotolo." I looked down on the coffee table and picked up the first photo Hughes had taken from the folder and said, "This is his father, Vinnie Sr. Damn that man could cook. It was such a shame when he passed away," Hughes' face lit up with acceptance. The other agent in the room was anxious to hear more. "Could you name these other men? Put the ones you've spent time on this side of the table and the ones you've seen in passing on the other side." "Sure, some of them I've spent plenty of time with. I even know their wives and children's names," I said. As I took out photos I gave them name after name of mob member and their family. Hughes nodded to the unnamed agent and was excited. "She knows them. She knows them all," he said. Then he turned to me and said, "Joie, what made you call us? Why reach out to the FBI?"

With a mixture of sadness and vengeance I told him the whole story of how I'd been scorned by Gino and the Mafia. I told him of the mistreatment we went through and how we had been left without food and money. I told him how we had been rejected by our own kind. "Fuck the Mafia. They left me and my daughter to starve. I want revenge," I said. "Joie, make a list of your financial needs and we will oblige them," said Hughes. "The Federal Bureau of Investigation will take care of you and your daughter." Now that I knew the Feds wanted me and what I had to offer I was ready to get to work. I wrote down a figure on a scrap of paper and slid it across the table to Hughes. He picked it up and said "Done!" "Gentlemen, get your pens ready then because what you're about to hear will be of great interest to you," I boasted. For hours we went back and forth in conversation. *Who's bringing the stuff in? Who's running the boats? Who's working the casinos? When are the planes flying and where are they located? What banks are they using? Who's in Chicago? Who's in Miami? Where are they purchasing the properties from? Where are the cars?* They asked question upon question and I gave them answer upon answer. Whatever I could give them I did and it was coming at a big price tag. Then they asked me a question that I never thought I would hear. "Joie, would you consider working undercover for us?" Hughes asked. "If you want me undercover, it's going to cost you a lot of money. I'm talking about serious coinage. We're not talking about thousands of dollars, we're talking big cash flow in exchange for me risking my life," I said. "I'm confident you'll be worth every penny, Joie," Hughes said with a smirk. "Is it okay if we get in contact with you tomorrow morning for a little bit more questioning?" "Listen, I'll do whatever you want but I'm not stepping foot in to the Federal Building until I see some cash," I said it so directly that Hughes knew not to try and pull anything over on me. "Okay Joie, we'll set everything up for you. We're the good guys, I promise you can trust us." "I don't believe shit until I see it," I was so frank that both agents laughed at my candid nature. All of the finer things in life I had were given to me later by the FBI and then some for my hard work and dedication. It was a greater pay off then I ever seen with the Mob.

The next day two agents of the FBI came to pick me up. Their names were Steve Hazel and Jim Brown. For some reason, I really felt that they should have had nicknames to use because the ones on their business cards were pretty dull. They drove me to an out of the way Embassy Suites hotel. "Why are we here?" I asked. "The Bureau felt it best to keep a very low profile with you. We wouldn't want your cover blown before we even got started," was the response given by Hazel. It all seemed legit to me and either way Hughes kept his word, I wasn't entering the Federal Building. Brown came and opened up my car door. I followed closely behind him to a room where they had laid out a breakfast feast. There was a long table covered in electronic devices. "What's all of this for is someone gonna DJ?" I joked. "Joie, so happy to see you again," said Hughes coming from the back of the room. "All of this equipment has been set up so we can keep record of everything you tell us. Allow me to introduce you to everyone," he said and led me around the room. "You already know these guys, Steve and Jim. I hope they weren't too boring on the ride here," he teased. "Very funny Hughes," said Hazel. He led me over to a man who was busy fixing a plate of food for himself. "This guy right here is Joe Tradowski," he said. "And these two are Andrew Thompson and Bob Levinson. They're going to be asking you some questions and taking notes. Thank you again for doing this. The Bureau is going to uphold their end of the bargain and make sure you and your daughter, Nikki, are well provided for," he said. So far he kept his word to me and I didn't have much of a reason not to trust him but every woman knows all men lie at some point. "Joie, before we begin I have to ask you a question," Levinson looked like he was ready to get down to business. I have seen that look one too many times working with the Mob. "Joie, do you feel you and your daughter will need witness protection from the Mafia. We can ensure your safety," he said with an honest expression of concern. "Listen, I'm not afraid of them. If the Mafia wanted me dead I would have been taken out a long time ago. My friends, *Smith and Wesson* have me covered with their .38 special and 9mm," I said. In all honesty, I had hoped one of those sonuvabitches from the Mafia would have come after me. With the way I felt, I was ready to settle the score and take them out. Everything was stolen from me. Everything I worked hard to build was destroyed. My money, my home, my life was all ripped away from me. Hell has no worse fury then a pissed off woman. If they tried to pull the trigger in my direction, they better not have missed because I would have made sure to hit my target.

"Okay then, let's begin," said Thompson. They started asking me questions about my life with Gene. They wanted details on how we met and how I came to be a part of things. They inquired about Hyman Larner and Noriega and what I may have known regarding their business relationship. They wanted to know more about Sal and Carmine Bastone. They touched on Santo Trafficante and my interactions with him. For hours, I sat and told them what they wanted to know. I went through photographs. I provided names of family members. If I wasn't worth anything to the Mafia then I wasn't keeping any of their secrets anymore. I gave them addresses to banks I used to launder money from and to the apartments where they entertained Noriega and other head honchos. I told them where they could find the plane used to transport guns, drugs and money over to Panama. I made sure they knew the hangar code and the identifying markings on the wing of the plane. I told them as long as they paid I would give them what they wanted.

One situation the FBI wanted to know more about was the double murder of Vinnie Ruotolo's parents. I told them what I had heard about the robbery at the hotel and Gene's involvement in the murders. I also divulged to them that Gene kept a secret ledger that contained information the Feds would be doing back flips over but I never told them it was in my possession. I considered the book to be my "ace-in-the-hole" if anything ever happened. Since Gino displayed no loyalty to me at the lawyers and demonstrated I meant nothing to him, I gladly returned the favor by letting the truth come out.

*Later on in months, I found out the FBI attempted to question Gene regarding his involvement in the murders but he had already passed away. Gene's family didn't bother to let Nikki nor myself know about his death. They didn't want us at the funeral. Nikki was devastated that she never had the chance to say goodbye and pay her proper respects. It didn't surprise me since Gene's family demonstrated that they had no class. Though I had turned my back on him, much like he did to me, I still felt like I owed one final thing to Gene. I went home and burned the ledger. I let it all turn to ashes just like our lives together. As the flames consumed the book, I knew it was a fitting way to say goodbye.*

My first official mission with the Feds led me to Chicago where they had a team waiting for me. My instructions were to set up a meeting with Sal Bastone and get whatever I could out of him. It seemed easy enough and I got a brand new Louis Vuitton purse complete with its' own recording device out of it. A girl's best friends are her accessories. Thanks to the Mafia, I learned how to keep my friends close but my enemies closer. My meeting with Sal did two good things for me. The first was it showed the G-men that I was willing to risk everything to give them what they wanted. The second was I had the opportunity to sit and look him in the face and smile while my knife was burying deep in his back. I knew both Gino and Santo would be turning over in their graves for my betrayal of our kind but I considered this war. Only the strong was fit to survive.

Satisfied with my service, the FBI arranged another mission for me immediately since I was already in Chicago. It was arranged for me to meet with a federal agent that had gone undercover in the Mafia at Mercy Hospital on Michigan Avenue. It was amazing to me how the G's loved to play both sides of the fence just as much as the Mafia did. Since I was in town, I decided to kill two birds with one stone and contacted one of my connections. While the Feds took care of setting the stage for me to meet their guy, I took a stroll through the hospital's cafeteria and met up with mine. During our lunch meeting, we discussed the "family business" and Gino. For the first time, I felt like an outsider looking in. As we were coming to the end of our meeting, Bob Levinson walked through room and gave me a signal. Even though he was a federal agent, it was nice to see his familiar face. I knew it was show time. I said good bye to my acquaintance and headed towards the elevator where Bob was waiting for me. "Who was that?" he asked. "Just a friend," I replied knowing he was fishing for something more from me. "Joie, you gotta be careful out here," he said. "Why Bob are you scared someone is going to take advantage of little old me or are you jealous?" I teased him. I saw his smirk on his face as he shook his head. "Dames," he said. I couldn't help but let out a hearty laugh as we stepped inside the elevator and headed to the third floor. "You owe me a steak dinner for that one," I joked.

As I approached the hospital room, I saw the agent I was supposed to meet with sitting in the bed with a gown on. He was posing as a patient. I sat in the chair alongside of his bed and examined the room. I was looking for the bugs that were planted by the feds to capture our conversation. I was a little leery about the situation because I knew as easily as I turned against the Mafia, this agent could turn against the Feds and rat us all out but I stuck it out. I was here with the FBI all over the hospital. I knew if something went down they would step in. Plus, I never went anywhere without packing heat so I kept my purse close to me. The agent started speaking to me, at first I was tuning him out until he started mentioning names that I knew all too well. When my ears heard the words, "The Old Man" and "Gene Talarico," I knew it was time to chime in. Having my full on attention, we discussed in details business matters that the two were involved with Noriega. I gave them information about the "coffins," Larner's glass house and apartments used back in Miami for Noriega's family. I knew the G's were trying to go for a large bust in narcotics and guns. The facts I was providing to them was worth its' weight in gold. When our conversation was over, I was brought to a waiting room while Bob Levinson and his team went in to recover the recording devices. I happened to look in to the hallway as the agent I met with walked past in his normal clothes. Appearances truly can be so deceiving.

"Okay Joie, we're done here," said Bob as he poked his head in to the room. I gathered my belongings up and was ready to get the hell out of there. Walking down the hallway to the elevators Bob said, "Listen, I know I owe you a steak dinner but how do you feel about a baseball game? I have some tickets and want to check it out before we go back to Florida." My senses began to tingle all over my body. Who did he know in Chicago to get tickets to a baseball game last minute? Not wanting to give my suspicion away just yet I said, "A baseball game huh? Sure, why not?" Being a soldier with the Mob, I learned never to underestimate someone or his/her intentions. For all I knew, Levinson could have been paid to take me out. The Mafia had all kinds of agents on the inside bought at high prices. As we stepped off the elevator, I told Bob I would meet up with him in a half hour at the hotel. I made an excuse that I wanted to change clothes and freshen up a bit before the game. "Okay Joie. Thanks for being a sport," he said. "More than you know," I teased. With the little bit of time I bought myself, I went back to my hotel room and changed in to something more comfortable which would nicely conceal the .38 nickel plated Smith and Wesson that I had attached to my ankle. My mother always did say accessories made the outfit. I took an extra second to touch up my make-up and was on my way to meet back up with Bob.

Stepping in to the lobby, I saw him through the glass doors outside smoking a cigarette. "Hey you," I said as I approached him. "I'm ready. Where's the car?" I asked. "We're gonna take the L," he said. "You wanna go on the subway?" suspiciously I asked. "Sure, when in Rome," he replied. Everything in my mind was telling me I wasn't making it back home to Nikki. I felt that I was going to be taken out in Chicago by this man and he was leading me to the slaughter. Walking towards the subway station, I noticed it was getting dark and gloomy. What a fitting setting, I thought to myself. I didn't bother to speak; I just let him lead the way while I tried to catch my breath. The subway car pulled up and we took our seats next to each other. There were not many passengers on board. The car looked dirty and it was covered in many coats of graffiti. I noticed one of the lights kept flickering on and off while a humming sound played what I felt would be the music to my last moments alive. The doors to the L closed and I felt my face grow hot from nervousness. *This is it. This is how it's going to end.* Sensing my paranoia, Bob said, "Joie, what's wrong with you? You seem nervous." "I'm fine," I said trying to play it cool. "Don't worry Joie. I got this with me," he said while reaching in his jacket to grab his 9mm pistol. I lifted my pant leg and displayed my .38 taped to my ankle. "Don't think for a second I'm worried," I said to him. We both were staring long and hard at each other. "I'm a federal agent Joie." "I don't give a fuck. The Feds have taken plenty of payoffs in the past. I don't trust anyone. If I'm about to go, you're going down with me," I stated my case point blank to him. The lights from the subway car flickered again. "Put your leg down Joie. Let's go and enjoy the game," Bob said shaking his head. "I would enjoy it better if the Yankees were playing with Ron Darling as the pitcher," I said. "Not much of a baseball fan, are you?" Bob said jokingly. We stepped off the L and headed towards the stairs that led to the street above the station. It was so serene to see Wrigley's Stadium in front of us. Even Bob took a moment to soak up the surroundings. Both of us were feeling the warmth of the people on the streets heading in to the stadium. As we took our seats, a woman in the same row sitting next to Bob leaned over and whispered in his ear. He let out a chuckle and said, "thank you." "What did she say to you?" I asked curious to find out. "She asked me if you were my wife. I shook my head yes to play along. Then she said you have the biggest rock she ever saw in her life on your hand!" After all the paranoia from the train, it felt good to let out a laugh.

*That day was the last time I saw Bob Levinson. I had inquired about him several times while working with the Federal Bureau of Investigations. The official story was he had an unsanctioned mission for the CIA in Iran and went missing in Kish Island in 2007. From my connections in the underground world, I found out he had been captured as a prisoner. Videos of him were leaked in 2010 and 2011 to prove that Bob was still alive. His family has gone on television and has made it known they believe the government has abandoned any actions to bring him home safely. From working first hand with Bob, I know he's strong enough to survive anything. I still pray one day he will be back on American soil and in the arms of his wife.*

Joie Miami

## Chapter Thirteen: The End is Near

It was 1991, after several successful missions with the FBI, their confidence in my abilities and information had grown. They knew I was legit and asked for me to go undercover again. This time they wanted me to join up with the Narcotics Unit of the Organized Crime Division. It didn't take long to find out why I was requested. An old and unfriendly acquaintance, Tommy Risotto, was back on radar. For months the Miami office and the Chicago team worked together to capture surveillance of Tommy and his soldiers but nothing was too solid to bust him. They needed me to go in and hit up some of my connections to see if I could help build their case.

"It's a lot for you to risk Joie. We know this and if you can't handle it let us know," said Frank Morrocco. "Frank you know me, when do I turn down a good time?" I said in a joking manner. "This one is going to require you to get in contact with some of your old school friends," he said. "I'll be sure to bring the bubbly," I teased. Agent Hughes came in the office with his nose buried deep in a folder of paperwork. "Hey boss," he said to Morrocco. "I'm sorry I'm late," he said with a look of frustration on his face. "It's ok

Dean," he said reassuringly. "Joie, what are you doing here?" Hughes asked. "She's going to be helping us on the Risotto case. What's going on with the other one you were assigned with the Costello guy? Have you found him yet?" Morrocco asked. "I visited all his old hang outs. I paid a visit to his last employer. I spoke with family. No one seems to know where he is," Dean replied. "Who are you looking for?" I asked. "Joie I know you've always been a reliable source of intelligence but I think this one might even stump you!" "Show me a picture of the guy and I'll tell you if I know him," I said. Hughes sat the folder down and took out a photograph of a familiar face. "This is the guy?" I asked. "Yeah, we've been looking for him for months and no one seems to know where he's at. It's like he disappeared from the face of the earth," Morrocco said. I looked at Hughes and asked, "do you happen to have a pen?" He reached in his jacket pocket and pulled out a Bic and handed it to me. I took a piece of scrap paper from the desk and wrote down an address to a bar called *Streamers*. Handing the paper to Hughes I said, "Be there at eight o'clock. He'll be at the bar." "Holy shit Joie! Do you really know *everybody* in Miami?" Hughes said. "Of course she does. That's why she's *Joie Miami*," Morrocco said. I took their words as compliments and cracked a big smile. "Well what are you standing around for?  Grab your team and get them ready to get Costello," Morrocco said to Hughes.

Stepping off the plane back in Shy Town, I could feel something different in the air.  I couldn't put my finger on it, but I didn't have that same welcoming feeling as I did when I was there with Bob Levinson.  It felt cold and the wind was giving me a great demonstration as to why it was called the "Windy City."  The Narcotics team sent me and a few of their best agents from Miami to Chicago to try and close up the Bastone case.  Word had kicked up that there was going to be a large shipment of pharmaceuticals going out.  We were there to find out when and where so the Feds could shut down shop.  If I knew anything about Tommy, he was going to give the G's one helluva fight.  He was a vicious bastard and would slit his own mother's throat if he was ever given the opportunity to so these agents would be easy pickings.  I knew I had to watch my back on Tommy's turf.  I never liked him nor did I have any respect for that bastard.

A black van pulled up outside of the airport terminal, the driver got out and helped with the luggage.  Seeing the black van with tinted windows, I felt like I was undercover for the Mob not the Feds.  "Where are we off to?"

an agent asked as we all got inside the vehicle. "Your accommodations are set up at the Holiday Inn downtown," said the driver. "Shit, what happened to the Embassy Suites?" I said. "We're a smaller division out here, so we get the crappy digs first," said a female agent. As the van came to a stop outside of the Holiday Inn, I went to grab my luggage. The feeling that someone was watching me washed completely over my body. I took a look around and couldn't see anyone but I knew that didn't mean they weren't there. I kept scouring the area and the cars surrounding the streets. "Come on Joie," said Hughes. "Let's go get checked in." He noticed I was looking around and said "What's wrong?" "I don't know. I got the feeling that someone is watching us," I said. "You sure?" he said and glanced over everything too. "I don't see anyone. Maybe it's from the long flight? I bet if you went to your room and took a hot shower you'd feel better." "Yeah, okay," I responded. A hot shower did sound pretty good at the moment.

Settling in to the hotel room, I turned the television on to see some of the local news. It was more so that the room didn't seem so quiet. I always hated traveling alone. With Nikki around, there was never a dull moment. I really did not like being away from her. I started the shower in the bathroom to let the steam fill up the room. I had just stepped inside and felt the warm water hit my flesh when I heard my hotel room phone ring. I let it go to voicemail. Enjoying the relaxing sensation of the steam and liquid on my body I took my time in the shower. It didn't take too long before I was disturbed by a knock at my room door. I grabbed my robe and towel and wrapped myself up to answer the door. I peeked through the peep hole and seen it was Hughes. "What's up?" I said after opening the door. "I'm sorry Joie. I didn't mean to disturb you. We're ordering dinner and the other team wanted to know if you would like something." "Oh okay, yeah I wouldn't mind some food. Give me a few minutes and I'll be right there. That's why you must have called the room," I said. "Call the room? We just got in. I don't know anyone's extensions yet. Sorry, it wasn't me," said Hughes innocently. "I'll go tell the others you'll be with them to place your order in just a few minutes," he said and turned to leave down the hallway. What Hughes had said about not knowing anyone's extensions struck me a little funny because he was right we all just got here. None of the team was given anyone's extensions. I looked over at the phone and saw there was a blinking red light. Someone left a voicemail for me. Following the instructions on the side of the phone, I pressed the buttons to retrieve my message. I sat on the side of the bed and heard, "Get the fuck out of Chicago bitch!" Suddenly my blood ran cold. I knew someone was watching me earlier. Tommy must have had someone on the inside tip him off that I was coming to help on his capture. My thoughts turned to the team I was with. Out of all of them the only one I could rule out as a rogue agent was Hughes. He had always kept his word to me and I had no real reason not to trust him. I knew I had to keep the voicemail to myself. I couldn't display any emotion over it or tell anyone. If there was a mole on the team, I wanted to find out who and let them know I didn't take kindly to threats and intimidation tactics. I knew I had to keep my eyes and ears open and stay on my underground connections to remain a step ahead. I also knew better then to go anywhere without my trusty .38 taped to my ankle.

Once we finished dinner, the team got right down to business. A chalk board was brought in and set up to keep track of information obtained. Photographs were taped to the walls of those known to associate with Tommy and his crew. Video surveillance was watched and recording were listened to. At one point, I was asked to listen to the tapes a second time to see if I could identify anyone or translate what was being said with Mafia terminology. I didn't mind, it was killing time, plus it gave me a chance to check out the other agents and feel them out. After several long hours of going over all the data and recordings, the team called it a night.

The next morning, I was up early to take advantage of the continental breakfast and coffee the hotel was serving. I was reading the morning paper and the feeling that someone was watching me came over me again. I casually put the paper down and scanned the room. I was looking to see if anyone may stick out or if I could catch the corner of an eye pointing my way. A bus boy came over and asked if he could clear any of my plates. I told him to go ahead. I was done and ready to leave anyway. Before I could get up, Hughes sat down at my table with a plate of fresh eggs and pancakes. "Where did you come from?" I asked. "I was just informed there's a continental breakfast here by the wonderful woman at the front desk." I watched Hughes eat last night during dinner. He definitely knew how to pack away the food and took no prisoners in his eating. "So you ready for today?" he asked. "As ready as I can be. I have a few connections I'm going to be contacting to see what they know. I'm also going to see what I can find out on the street," I said. "Mind if I tag along? I know you can handle yourself. This team out here just isn't as friendly as I would have liked them to be," said Hughes almost like he was looking for sympathy. Normally, I would have been a bitch and said no but I knew he wasn't lying. This team didn't have the same couth as the last one I worked with. "Sure why not. I could use a trustworthy team mate," I said. As Hughes sat and shoveled his food in to his mouth, I was busy thinking about that voicemail from the night before. I didn't recognize the voice as being someone from the team or anyone I used to associate with. Tommy must have found some street punk and had him call me so I couldn't tell who it was. I was more annoyed then I was scared. I knew I was in shark infested waters and was waiting to see the fins.


After breakfast, Hughes and I went looking for the other members of the Chicago team we were supposed to rendezvous with. We went in to the lobby and a front desk clerk called us over to the desk. "Are you Agent Hughes?" she asked. "I sure am," he said with a flirtatious smile. "One of the other agents left this for you," she said and handed him an envelope. "Thank you." He opened it and there was a handwritten note giving him the address to the Chicago FBI headquarters. "Joie, it looks like we have to meet up with the team downtown. There must be something big about to go down," he said. "Alright let's get going," I told him and headed towards the lobby doors. Stepping outside in to the sunlight, I could see a car parked across the street with someone looking in our direction. Making eye contact, the driver put the car in reverse and peeled off. "What the hell was that?" asked Hughes. "Company," I said. "We need to move now!" I told him and started moving quickly towards the street. I knew the best thing to do would be just to keep going and not stay still. Agent Hughes was keeping up with my pace. I had that feeling that something serious was about to happen. Tommy had always been known to be silent but deadly. I knew if his crew was involved I would have to stay alert. I bent down and took my gun from my ankle. "Joie, what are you doing? There are civilians everywhere," he said. "Are you crazy? Do you know what's going through the thoughts of Tommy and his men? They already know we're here and I for one am not going to be an easy target!" I said. "What do you mean they know we're here?" Hughes was confused. "I had a message left on my hotel phone telling me to get out of Chicago. These aren't men that are going to sit and play hide and seek with you. They're going to try to take someone out and I don't plan to be that person," I said. "Okay Joie. Okay. I trust you. What do we do now?" he asked. "Keep an eye out. They are still here. I can feel them watching us," I said. Out of the corner of my eye, I spotted two hoods getting out of a tan colored Oldsmobile. They were both tall. One was heavy set and looked kind of like a gorilla in his size. The other was thin but looked like he could still keep up with anything that might play out. They were both definitely not two guys I would like to meet in a dark alley on a late night. They kept their heads low and were heading in our direction fast. The thin one had his hand inside of his jacket. I knew he was reaching for his pistol. Hughes spotted them too. "Get behind me Joie," he said. I shot a glance in his direction. "What the hell are you doing?" I said. "I'm trying to protect you from whatever is coming this way," he said. "Don't worry. I'm not scared," I said with a smirk across my face and cocking my pistol, "the best is yet to come!" Agent Hughes took out his pistol and looked me hard in the eyes. "Alright Joie, ladies first!" Raising my loaded gun to just the right height I took a deep breath and said, "Don't mind if I do."

Made in the USA
Middletown, DE
22 August 2015